When the
Balls Drop

When the
Balls Drop

How I Learned to Get Real
and Embrace Life's Second Half

Brad Garrett

G

Gallery Books
New York   London   Toronto   Sydney   New Delhi

G

Gallery Books
An Imprint of Simon & Schuster, Inc.
1230 Avenue of the Americas
New York, NY 10020

First Gallery Books hardcover edition May 2015

GALLERY BOOKS and colophon are registered trademarks of Simon & Schuster, Inc.

For information about special discounts for bulk purchases, please contact Simon & Schuster Special Sales at 1-866-506-1949 or business@simonandschuster.com.

The Simon & Schuster Speakers Bureau can bring authors to your live event. For more information or to book an event, contact the Simon & Schuster Speakers Bureau at 1-866-248-3049 or visit our website at www.simonspeakers.com.

Interior design by Jill Putorti

Manufactured in the United States of America

10 9 8 7 6 5 4 3 2 1

Library of Congress Cataloging-in-Publication Data is available.

ISBN 978-1-4767-7290-5
ISBN 978-1-4767-7292-9 (ebook)

To my children Max and Hope,
with love and adoration.

When the
Balls Drop

Being Forward

My decision to write this book, and the inspiration for its title, came as the result of an experience I had shortly after my fifty-third birthday. I had gotten up to take my third piss of the night . . . like I do every night. I had actually learned how to navigate to the bathroom in complete darkness, thanks to my slightly enlarged prostate. I sat down to pee. Yes, that's right, I sat to pee, for a few reasons. (Rednecks, laugh here.) For one, I'm circus-freak tall, and balance at two A.M. when I'm half asleep is not to be taken for granted. Two, aim has never been my forte. And three, I'm a bit OCD, and I didn't want to spend the rest of the night on all fours with a can of Lysol, trying to figure out where the misfires landed. So I decided to sit my jumbo can down to cut my losses.

As a side note, I'd like to propose that aim is more mathematical than we tend to acknowledge. For me, it's: smallish dick ÷ long torso = distance to bowl^2. And for those of you who don't know, your early fifties are when your strong single stream of whiz morphs into several unevenly dispersed rivulets, like a sprinkler that was backed over by a mower. In my case, there are four unruly streams: the one on my far right was apparently designed with the sole purpose of hitting the roll of toilet paper; next to that is Mr. Noodle, who prefers to dribble straight down onto my foot; then there's the second-to-the-left stream, which reminds me of my youth as it arcs high enough to hit the fuzzy toilet seat cover; and last but not least, my far-left offender, who doesn't show up until my junk is put away and I'm driving to work in my new khakis. It's crucial to understand that at this point in a man's life, his "one-eyed liar" is no longer his friend, so guys, erase that from your happy place.

The moment I sat down on the john, I noticed something alarmingly different. Something I had never felt in my fifty-three years on earth. I became aware that the very bottom of my balls was wet. Thaaat's right. Not damp or overheated but *wet*. My middle-aged mind was trying to think back. Could I have been sleepwalking and done a snow angel on my Los Angeles lawn only to return to bed and continue my slumber? Could I have pissed myself while dreaming about the chocolate rugelach at Bea's Bakery? Unlikely. After all, my sheets weren't wet, and if I'd already released the hounds, I wouldn't have needed to get up to pee. For the third time.

The harsh reality is that my sequestered twins are advancing in the opposite direction of my earhair. Mother Nature has me by the balls, literally. They have actually started a race with my ex-wife's tits. And she will prevail, because she will get hers "done" as I continue to disappear into the abyss of recycled toilet brine. In the end, gravity always wins, people. Remember: when you have a heart attack, you fall down, not up.

Middle age is upon me, and I don't remember this shit being in the brochure. I have six different doctors on speed dial, and the font size on my smartphone is at ten with a maximum setting of twelve. That doesn't give me much wiggle room for the golden years.

Now, before your denial causes you to throw this book away or use it to flatten out your coupons for Metamucil, please remember that being a comedian allows me to have a more realistic, if not darker, outlook on life, death, aging, hookers, marriage, parenting, travel, premature ejaculation, politics, religion, race, and evolution in general. Add the Jewish component to that equation, and the outlook becomes even bleaker. My people usually have their burial plots picked out by the age of twenty-one, and they try to reserve them in the vicinity of their passed-on relatives whom they've hated for most of their lives. Guilt after death, I suppose. Personally, I want to be cremated and sprinkled in with "Love My Carpet" in the "Pardon my Pet" scent, and then vacuumed up by an illegal Filipino in a sundress. That's right, illegal. Because that adds to the danger.

Don't judge me yet. You have many more chapters to do that.

✿   ✿   ✿

After inhabiting this odd planet for over half a century, I've discovered the only thing I know for sure is that middle age is the window to your eventual end, and the view is often foggy, with sporadic flashes of light that could be the Lord, a bus to Atlantic City, the cops, or the beginning of a stroke. This book is not meant to be depressing, it's meant to be *liberating*, because it's written through the eyes of an optimistic pessimist. The boneheaded and self-absorbed pseudo-optimist will be familiar with disappointment, whereas the realistic pessimist has the luxury of being pleasantly surprised.

There are those of you who may choose to live in a dream world where the glass is half full, but if you do, you're an imbecile. The glass will never be half full. Nor full ever again. It's simply on its way to empty. It's half empty, three-quarters empty, then totally fucking empty. Pretty much like your upcoming golden years, if you don't start catching my drift. When you turn fifty, are you halfway to death or halfway to birth? Point made.

I feel it's my job as the village idiot to prepare the townspeople the best way I can: through honest observation that their chances of getting to old age without making at least one stinky in their pants while shopping at Target is very unlikely. If you try to oversteer the inevitable course of life, you will ruin the journey. I know that sounds like a crock of shit, and it is, but it's my book. And please understand, the moral of this story is not just about giving up the crap that continues to disappoint, it's also about me helping you. Using my high school education and suburban street smarts, I can teach you that by simply letting go of the bullshit that's been drummed into your brain by others, you shall experience a newfound freedom that comes with not giving a damn. Because if you haven't noticed, the clock is ticking, hombre.

It's my sincere goal that the following helps you to better understand what midlife is truly about. Or at least not to feel alone in your unexpected discoveries. Because being hated by your teenagers, misunderstood by your coworkers, fearful of the latex glove, unloved by your significant other, forgetful when shopping, achy when laughing, tortured by your ex, constipated while on a cruise (or on land), intrigued by younger, pretty counterparts and other parts is all par for the course. With more of the same shit to come. The good news: we're all in this together.

And when you factor in my limited vocabulary, the large font, wide margins, and photos throughout, this book should be a swift read.

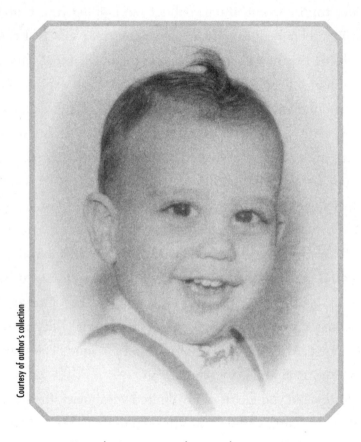

My mother's sonogram in her second trimester, 1960.

I Was a Ten-Pound Preemie

As stated earlier, I am a pessimistic optimist, or what I like to call a "pissed-omist." This is a person who has lived long enough to know not to expect much from most people or life in general, but still allows him- or herself the hope that somewhere under all the horseshit there may possibly be a pony. As you'll see, there were many factors that influenced the theories, neuroses, and occasional lunacy that inspired this book, and I feel you deserve the inside track. Therefore, please bear with me as I give you a bit of insight into my life to improve your understanding of how I arrived at this particular mentality.

I was born Brad H. Gerstenfeld on April 14, 1960, to Alvin from the Bronx, New York, and Barbara from Bellingham, Washington. I tipped the scales at nine pounds, eleven ounces. My dad never knew what the H in my name stood for, and my mother didn't tell me until I was twenty that it stood for Harry, after her favorite uncle. The birth certificate just says "H." If she was that embarrassed about the name, why the hell would she give it to me? Spell it out or pick another.

"I was such a large sperm, my mother went into labor during conception." I wrote that joke when I was fifteen, which made sense considering my mother used to tell total strangers, "He was so huge at birth that the doctors wanted to break my pelvis or Brad's shoulders in order to get him out of me, but I insisted they just use the tongs." (She had trouble remembering the word "forceps.") To this day I don't know if that tool was actually used or not, but there are two tiny indentations on my skull that fill up with water when I sweat.

Every man's life (and a portion of my stand-up) revolves around the mystery that is his penis. In reality, without one, none of us would exist, so it deserves exploring. Let me start by saying that mine has never been right. Unfortunately, I think it all began with the rabbi, who must have had some resentment toward my family that he indirectly took out on me. My paranoia knows no bounds . . . Maybe the *mohel* just stank at his job, like most people. Or maybe he had ADD and found himself distracted by the mound of chopped liver formed into the shape of the Wailing Wall or the hubcap-size cheese Danish sweating on the buffet table.

I always found it so odd that people could eat immediately after seeing an infant's penis being mangled by a stranger in a black robe and sketchy beard. How can an act so visceral and cringe-worthy lead directly to food? Perhaps it's merely diversion, or nervous eating, or years of conditioning. It's probably the same mental disconnect by which Italians can dismember a body, dump it in the river, and then go for ribs. I suppose this is where the term "comfort food" originated.

The bottom line is my circumcision was fucked up. I have more of a two-skin. The Yid must have stopped the trimming somewhere in the middle. He bailed on my rehemming like a Vegas dealer suddenly asked to go on break. He clapped his hands, wished everybody luck, and left the cards where they were. It's no secret that when a circumcised penis is at rest, it appears as if the little fella is wearing a cozy turtleneck sweater, right? Not mine. It's as if my dick is wearing a hoodie. He looks like the smallest criminal on record. Like a little poker player with his head on his chips. Either way, I got ripped off. Literally. And it's made me second-guess my manhood my entire life.

My urologist, Dr. Spiegelman, who by the way is the only person not to pass out from laughter after I remove my pants, believes the size has nothing to do with the botched circumcision. He also tried to convince me that in my case, "the appearance of having a small penis is only an optical illusion because it is on a body of massive girth." Optical illusion? He actually brought up magic in a medical context to make me feel better. In other words, like in real estate: location, location, location. I suppose if my penis were on a Chinese fellow, it would look enormous. I will have to test that theory the next time I'm dining at Twin Dragon.

In addition to bad taste in *mohels,* my mom had a flair for drama. It went along beautifully with her Kabuki makeup and sequined outfits. She was like a Liza Minnelli imperson-ator without the gay husbands.

I'll never forget when I was six years old and I saw two dogs getting it on for the very first time. Bewildered and concerned, I blurted out, "Mommy, what's wrong with those two dogs?"

"Well, darling," she said after a considerable pause, "the dog in the front is very sick, and his friend is pushing him to the hospital." This obviously messed me up for years to come, because every time I injured myself, I would seek out the neighborhood dog in hopes of being led to the ER.

Regardless of what anyone believes, almost every guy marries someone either very close to his own mother or the complete opposite. This is why I've spent the majority of my adult life with women who are borderline comatose, for fear of being with someone who inadvertently breaks into "Don't Rain on My Parade" during a canoe ride.

When I was seven, my parents divorced. It was very difficult for me, but I felt worse for my older brothers, Jeff and Paul, whose biological father literally disappeared after divorcing my mother, never to show his loser face again. To this day, I cannot comprehend a parent who could walk out on his or her children. Some people are truly heartless and narcissistic enough to do such a thing, I suppose. I always felt bad that I had such an involved father and my brothers would never know theirs; even though my father adopted my brothers early on, their relationships were strained at best. You really couldn't blame my brothers, because how could they trust a father figure again, let alone one so quickly?

My dad was a six-foot-five handsome chap with tough good looks and piercing blue eyes. He also, unfortunately, happened to be bipolar. Back in that era, no one knew what bipolar was, so he was written off as moody, difficult, compulsive, and extravagant, with grandiose ideas of a better life that kept him in constant debt. But he was my hometown hero, and I desperately needed one. He always had my back regardless of the situation, and I loved him for that, although it didn't make for a realistic later life.

He used to say, "It's you and me against the world, kid," and as wonderful and comforting as that may have been at the time (especially considering I always felt very alone), it often made me wonder why the world was against us in the first place. I guess having several ex-wives can make you feel like you're on the run or that life is based on a "you versus them" mentality. But he was super-cool and different from most dads, with his Indian jewelry and antique cars. He was literally *the* greatest salesman who ever lived, and through his constant, sometimes manic drive, he was able to convince me that I could be anyone and do anything.

After the divorce was final, my mother moved us to an apartment in the San Fernando Valley. Soon after, she would start dating a gentleman whom she met over the phone. He was cold-calling parents of boys who were of bar mitzvah age off a list he got from the local temple, offering his services to provide music and entertainment for the upcoming event. His name was Lionel Ames, and he was known for being the town's most popular Jewish singer and bandleader, playing weddings and bar mitzvahs all around Southern California; once in a while he would play one of the local clubs on the Sunset Strip. He was every Jew broad's dream guy: handsome, a freelance cantor/balladeer, and he could sing the shit out of "My Yiddishe Mama." He also drove a purple Chevy Impala (though he swore it was blue), and I'm sure that gave him some Hasidic street cred.

Lionel would soon become my mom's third husband, just in time for my brother Paul's bar mitzvah. The entertainment was free. And Lionel became my closest link to anyone involved in the entertainment industry. Lucky for me, he shared every tidbit he could. It took a special man to marry my mom with three boys in tow, and he had his hands full attempting to maintain some stability in a very emotional (and often turbulent) household.

Throughout my childhood, my father tried to see me as often as possible, while also bouncing from one sales job to another. Over the course of his life, he worked as a stockbroker, owned a design studio, sold "questionable" land in the high desert, owned a pie restaurant, and spent twenty-two years selling hearing aids, among other things. He was a brilliant guy who could figure out my high school algebra homework even though he barely finished seventh grade. He had a photographic memory and a laugh that made you laugh. And he was funny as hell. Sure, he had swings like Benny Goodman, but not when it came to being a responsible father. Just about every weekend, I would stare out my bedroom window, waiting for his car to pull up, as it always would. As I grew older, I became more of a best friend and wingman than a son. As a teenager and young adult, I found this pretty exciting, but after a few more years of maturing into manhood, I realized it wasn't the healthiest of scenarios.

Our close bond meant that my dad recognized the toll their divorce was taking on me, and when I was nine, he introduced me to a child therapist. Nate was like a hip college professor who smoked a pipe, wore sleeveless sweaters, and drove an original yellow MINI Cooper. I had to leave my classroom every Thursday at ten A.M. to see him, and my excuse to all of my dumbfounded classmates was that I had a dentist appointment. They knew something else was going on, because in those days my teeth looked like hell, and who on earth has a dentist appointment every week? But in 1969, if a kid went to see a shrink, he had to be crazy, right? Life was already too shitty at school to let that one out of the bag, so I got the reputation as the kid who had to constantly go to the dentist. Which of course turned into "Gerstenfeld has like a hundred cavities . . ."

Nate and I would walk around the neighborhood and talk rather than sit in his office. One of his exercises for helping me conquer my extreme anxiety was to coerce me into stealing oranges from people's trees; years later, he admitted he just loved oranges. He was a compassionate and kind man when it came to communicating with children, and to this day we remain close friends. My father was always strained financially, and Nate told my dad he could pay for my sessions over time so I could continue with therapy. I never forgot that, because it made me feel that maybe I was worth something.

As grateful as I am for the positive aspects of my early years, there is no doubt the more troublesome ones left their mark. At three years old, even though I appear happy in photos, I already have bags under my eyes that look like

I'm burning the midnight oil while holding down two jobs to make ends meet. The bags have followed me throughout my life. They're my earned stripes, my medals of horror. They're from years of insomnia combined with my Semitic coloring, constant worrying, angry masturbation, my inability to roll with shit, fear of the Nielsen Family, feelings of inadequacy when showering, and the daily dread that comes with pursuing the American dream. Take it for what you will: nature or nurture. It wasn't always pretty, but it got me here.

2

Jews Don't Dribble

When you're a large kid, people always assume you're older than you are, and they tend to treat you as such. This comes with both an added pressure of expectation and some undeniable perks. The irony of age, of course, is that we want to appear older when we're young and younger when we're old, proving that the human species is rarely content with any stage of life. That is, until you experience the true bliss of total voluntary surrender—but I'll get to that later.

School was a nightmare for me straight through junior high. I was as tall as my teacher in the third grade, and by sixth grade, everyone thought I was an undercover narc or had flunked a couple of years. I always sat in the back of the class so as not to block the blackboard for the poor bastard sitting behind me.

Whenever teams were picked during PE, I was always second to last before Ronald Wulfson, who was known as "Planet" for obvious reasons. In dodgeball, I was always the first out because I was the biggest target. Having the speed of a sloth didn't help, either, so I had more welts on me from that fucking game than you could imagine. Those big red rubber balls that smelled like asphalt found their way to my head more often than not, and the asinine rule was that if you were beaned in the head, it didn't count and you weren't out. The shot had to be below the neck, meaning every whack to the noggin bought me another round of torture, in which I could only hope to take one to the dick for a change. It is for this same reason that I have zero desire to go to Israel. Seven-foot Jew equals Arab's wet dream. Just lob one over the wall and leave with any prize from the top shelf.

When I hit the six-foot mark at thirteen, I noticed the majority of the population was in denial with regard to my athletic potential. The townspeople refused to believe that I couldn't play ball. I would have killed to become a good basketball player, because that would have gotten me the acceptance I constantly craved. When I would tell coaches I could not play basketball, they needed to see it to believe it, thus adding to my angst and embarrassment. "All you have to do is jump, Gerstenfeld!" Coach Tuccimini would bellow as I lumbered up and down the cracked, blacktop courts at George Hale Junior High. My room was lined with posters of John Havlicek, Jerry West, and Lew Alcindor (the early Kareem) in hopes that they would give me extra motivation. No Jewish players in that lineup, you'll notice—Jews don't dribble until they get to be around eighty. I never heard a sportscaster yell, "Rebound by Robinowitz!"

I dreamed of becoming the next Wilt Chamberlain. He was the star center of the Los Angeles Lakers at the time. My dad told me stories about how he would see Wilt every now and then leaving a nightclub with two or three women at a time. For this reason alone, I wanted to wake up black and buffed, with a penis that required a spotter when erect—not to mention a stealth hook shot to beat the Celtics at the buzzer.

I wanted so desperately to own Wilt's trademark gold headband, but every sporting goods store was sold out of them. So I decided to cut the waistband off of my underwear, paint it gold, and wear it in my next pickup game at recess. I knew it would fit perfectly because I always wore my underwear on my head when I imitated my aunt Esther for my brothers. I was naive enough to think the other kids wouldn't be able to tell the difference; I thought if I colored the waistband correctly, I could fool everyone, even though it said "Waist 32" and "Fruit of the Loom" on it. Skip Goldwaser, the only Jew at my school with a jump shot, was onto me the minute I hit the court. The whispers started and the chuckles followed and I became officially known as "the giant loser who wore his underwear waistband on his head."

It was around this time that I decided to sport a mini Jewfro in hopes of, again, being more Wilt-like. I looked as if Herman Munster and Greg Brady had a child. I couldn't win. And to top it off, my mom was insistent on cutting my mop. "The Afro is not going to get points with the Latin students, darling. You have enough trouble already with the whites," she said as we waited in the drive-through for tacos at Jack in the Box. What the hell was she talking about? What Latins? I think she meant Latinos, or perhaps she was confusing Latin with Latin Americans. Either way, she wanted the 'fro gone.

What I think puzzled me even more back then was that Jack in the Box sold two tacos for thirty-nine cents. Not one but *two* tacos. This was baffling to me, because gum was forty cents and didn't contain beef. Or at least what we thought was beef. How did they do it? What part of the cow could they sell for thirty-nine cents? This shit kept me up at night. In more ways than one.

My dad sided with me to convince my mom to leave my hair alone. He had a mini-fro as well. But to my mom, it showed disrespect to wear your hair long. I wanted to be like my two older brothers, with long, cool, wavy hair, love beads, and bell-bottoms. When I tried to pull off that look, it was not kind. I looked like a tranny at a luau.

It's odd how men have a very deep connection to their

hair that I can only assume goes back to the prehistoric days, when we were forced to camouflage among other furry land dwellers in hopes of not being devoured. The shit guys go through to save their fuzz is insane. Just think of James Taylor, Sean Connery, and Bruce Willis. You think they have trouble getting laid? Let it go, gentlemen.

My mom always cut our hair herself with a device called the Hair Whiz, which she bought from a late-night television commercial. It was pretty much like a straight razor with a plastic handle. I think it was originally designed to shear sheep or cut upholstery. No matter how we pleaded, we all got a variation of an accidental mullet. I recall once running away from home the day before I was supposed to get my hair cut. I'll never forget the bravery it took as I closed my eyes and jumped down nineteen inches from my bedroom window onto a cushy patch of succulents. We had a one-story house. I guess walking out the front door wouldn't have been as dramatic as doing a tuck-and-roll onto plush landscaping. To me, it might as well have been an escape from Terminal Island: I ran for dear life in broad daylight (Jews don't run away if it's dark out) to the market three miles down the hill, where I called my dad from a pay phone. He drove all the way from downtown as I hid in the produce section of Vons. When he picked me up we went to have some pie at Marie Callender's, like we always did, and he told me about the importance of sticking up for what I believed in, which included preserving my Afro.

We loved pie. We bonded over it. Marie Callender's was like our clubhouse. And one day my dad would buy a franchise called House of Pies that almost drove him to an early grave. He had to do most of the baking from midnight to five in the morning and had no idea what he was doing. He sold it in two years and lost a bundle.

It should come as no surprise that I was bullied beyond belief, and once the smaller guys knew I wasn't great at fighting back, I became fair game for a large part of the student body. That's when I discovered the Goon Squad: a gaggle of oddities who ran in a pod consisting of fat kids, brainiacs, those with special needs (evident or not), loners, nerds, redheads, and kids who freely ate boogers in public. I was immediately elected president of the Island of Misfit Toys because I had the loudest voice in all of Platt Ranch Elementary, and my screams for help could be heard across the schoolyard. I was Foghorn Leghorn with abandonment issues. And I became the resident comic of this group because I had the ability to ease our dread of inferiority by secretly making fun of the bullies while also imitating our least favorite teachers. The goons needed some comic relief, and I needed an audience. I had found my niche.

My strategy from early on was always to draw the uncomfortable focus onto myself before others had time to point and ridicule. The idea is to beat the haters to the punch. In the same way that Quasimodo needed to run up to the bell tower and ring the shit out of the bells to gain even more attention (as if being a deformed hunchback wasn't enough), we must all make sure we draw attention to our flaws before others do. This is recommended for my diminutive counterparts as well. And large folks, listen up: don't stoop or slouch, because then you look like a Great Dane who just laid one out behind the couch. Stand tall but not too proud. Pride can make you look like a dick if you're not careful.

Hamming it up at my mom's third wedding, 1968.

3

Bitten

My turbulent and awkward childhood led me to devise a survival strategy, which was to try and become anyone but myself. Over the years I've noticed this is the same process that propels many people into show business. Ironically, it's the opposite of what we want to accomplish later in life. That's the delicate balancing act that most everyone struggles with: "Who the hell am I today? Right now? And are there any other choices available?"

In my earlier days as a stand-up, like the playground tactics that preceded them, my humor always leaned toward self-deprecation. There's still some of that today, but I think every comic, especially in the beginning, is fueled by his larger emotions or feelings about himself, which are almost always negative. That's why we're comics. These years also saw the birth of my irreverent sense of humor and my need to push the envelope in both personal and professional life. I chose not to be the typical giant who slumped over or hid in the corner or on top of the beanstalk. Instead, I decided to create a humor as loud and unfiltered as I was. Fortunately, this served me well in later life, because women love humor. It's a known fact that next to musicians and athletes, comics get laid the most. Luckily, comedians age much better than bass players or quarterbacks, so if you think you are truly funny, you can cancel your gym membership right now. Broads want to laugh, not fight you for the mirror.

My childhood dreams of becoming a fireman, policeman, or doctor were dashed by age nine when I could no longer fit into a youth-size Halloween costume for any of those occupations. It was as if I went from Casper to Richard Nixon overnight. (Even a few years ago I went to Party City to buy a costume to take my kids out trick-or-treating. I figured a clown was easy until I went to try on the clown feet. I couldn't get them on; they were too fucking small. They were three feet long, why the hell couldn't I get my size-fifteen flipper in there?)

I took a music class in school and toyed with the thought of becoming a flautist to offset my mammoth persona. Unfortunately, the smaller instruments went to the girls, and I was stuck with the baritone horn, one size under tuba. After one week of having to schlep my instrument home from school, a mile and a half uphill, I decided maybe I wasn't cut out to be a musician. I was diagnosed with a hernia three weeks into orchestra class. My doctor suggested not blowing hard for six weeks after the operation. He also advised that I not carry the large horn home for at least the same amount of time. I was moved into percussion, but unfortunately not the drums. I rotated from the triangle to cymbals depending on the holiday program.

To me and my dad, black musicians and artists were the epitome of cool. My dad was great at doing impressions and inspired me to venture into that realm also. Flip Wilson, Bill Cosby, and Jimmie Walker were the first in my arsenal. I'm slightly embarrassed to say that my first act, at fifteen, was an impersonation of Jimmie Walker. In blackface. As off-putting as that sounds, I need to inform you that my act was highly regarded on the bar mitzvah circuit, and the impression was so dead-on that I somehow got away with it. At the time, Jimmie was the biggest star in television on the show *Good Times,* and truly, it was done out of admiration and respect, however misguided.

On further consideration, it occurs to me that perhaps the screams of laughter were from the fact that I was walking into a temple in blackface, as opposed to my impression being great. I would recite the jokes off Jimmie's hit album, wearing his trademark jean hat and burgundy turtleneck. In hindsight, I guess I was lucky to have made it past my fifteenth birthday. I didn't find any of this to be racist, though I did find it racial and provocative and actually pretty damn funny. Especially to a kid who was being influenced by a new show called *Saturday Night Live*. To me, it was no different than when Eddie Murphy brilliantly portrayed the old Jewish men in his films or when Richard Pryor made fun of white people. The general population just wasn't used to white guys trying that kind of stuff.

As I look back on it today, I can't believe my utter fearlessness, my lack of propriety, and the balls I possessed in my teens. I also can't believe I was allowed to leave the house in friggin' blackface! My parents, who were very supportive of my comedy as well as very liberal, clearly didn't see the harm or offense. I was acting. Like Othello on weed, perhaps, but acting.

My cousin Darren and I, born nine days apart, grew up more like brothers, since his house was just down the street. When we had sleepovers, we would quietly turn on his television after bedtime to catch Johnny Carson's monologue on *The Tonight Show*. We would always make sure to catch the young comics: Robert Klein, David Brenner, Joan Rivers, Steve Landesberg, Martin Mull, and David Steinberg were the staples.

Then one night I caught Don Rickles on *The Tonight Show*, and my life changed forever. I couldn't believe what I was seeing. It was the first time I'd ever witnessed

Carson and Ed McMahon crying from laughter. Don was ruthless and hysterical. Jabbing Ed about his weight and boozing, and roasting Johnny about his marriages and salary. Making fun of the black guy in the band. Telling irreverent stories about his buddy Sinatra. There was a sense of discomfort when Rickles took to the stage that made everything even funnier because he was fearless and no one was safe. But his genius came from the audience knowing full well he didn't mean it.

After seeing Don perform, I knew for certain I wanted to pursue comedy as a career. I wanted to make folks laugh about themselves the same way I had to laugh about myself. To make everyone fair game no matter who they were. Ironically, it wasn't until later in life that I realized how much my comedic *style* was influenced by this middle-aged curmudgeon. I always felt like the put-upon outcast who wanted his day in court, and Rickles's humor made it okay to play the judge. One thing I was keenly aware of, however, was the fact that I had to make fun of myself before turning the tables on the audience. Rickles was short, bald, and pudgy. I was a giant with a big voice. If I didn't set it up right, I'd come off as nothing more than a bully. I would have to let the audience see my vulnerability, insecurity, and playfulness. They needed to know what really lay beneath my surface before I could be trusted to unload on them.

To this day, Rickles remains one of the few comics who commands reverence and adoration from every generation of stand-ups to follow. He's a true one of a kind. A few years ago in a packed restaurant in Malibu, Don walked up to my table and bellowed, "Hey, Garrett, let's put an escalator up your ass and make ya into a building!" Then he looked at my young girlfriend and said, "Whataya, twelve, honey? You been kidnapped? Just blink if you're kidnapped." Friggin' hilarious. It was one of the greatest nights of my life. Roasted by the King.

My first year in high school was when the stand-up in me really started to emerge; by senior year, it was well engrained. Being the lunchtime disc jockey at the school, I was chosen to MC a year-end event where various teachers were recognized by the student body as they sat on a dais. Having been raised on the Dean Martin Roasts, which I never missed, I had a few minutes of material on each teacher that was anything but flattering. As luck would have it, the teachers ate it up and the students went crazy, and I made it out alive with a much better idea of what I would do after I finished school.

Five days later, at my graduation from El Camino Real High School, class of 1978, the public address system used to announce each student during the procession went out just as they were starting on the G's. The families couldn't hear the names of their kids as they received their diplomas onstage. Since he knew I had the lungs of an off-key opera singer, the principal asked me to stand beside him and yell the names of the graduates as they appeared. We were outdoors, so my pipes probably only made it ten rows deep, but it was better than nothing, and the crowd loved it. Luckily, they got the PA system working again just before we hit the K's.

When I started to take myself seriously as a comic, one of the first steps I took in reinventing myself was to change my name, which I did at eighteen. Being born a Gerstenfeld (which means "barley field" in German), I went in search of a better handle. At age seventeen, I saw my name squeezed onto a tiny marquee during a talent contest at a dingy night-club on Ventura Boulevard called the Turkey Farm. I knew it was only a matter of time until the name had to go. I wanted to keep the G from my birth-given name as an homage to my Jewish heritage. Not really. I'm lying. I felt guilty about totally abandoning my namesake and didn't want to hurt my father's feelings, although he hated the name as well. Mostly I wanted to keep the G because I had just purchased a monogrammed robe. So I flipped through the phonebook and considered Garner and Gannon for a minute, and even Elliott, because I loved Elliott Gould. But Brad seemed to flow better with Garrett.

Looking back now, I wish I'd kept the barley field. The truth is, as I slide into middle age and desire more authenticity from myself, I don't feel Garrett when I look in the mirror. I feel Gerstenfeld. Especially as I begin to age and look more like my father. I think it's the ultimate acceptance that comes with aging that is most rewarding. Where "screw it" becomes a way of life as opposed to an attitude.

One of the aforementioned perks that came with looking years beyond my age was that I got to perform in the clubs before I was twenty-one. I had been doing stand-up off and on for about four years when my older brother Paul encouraged me to sign up for an open mic one night at the Comedy Store in Westwood. I drew a number that put me on around eleven-thirty P.M., which was not an ideal time slot for a Monday. Let's just say the crowd's reaction was worse than "crickets." I single-handedly took bombing to a new level: not just hearing crickets but actually hearing crickets' *thoughts*. Of course it's possible I did so poorly because of the genius I had to follow that fateful night: "A very funny guy who's starring in his own series on ABC. Ladies and gentlemen, Robin Williams!" the MC yelled.

Robin had recently exploded onto the scene from his starring role in *Mork & Mindy,* and the place became unglued as he took to the stage in his baggy pants and trademark rainbow suspenders. A wave of simultaneous nausea and elation came over me. I never missed his television show; he was a huge inspiration for me and just about every other budding comic at that time.

The audience was on their feet before he said a word, and suddenly, I couldn't feel my legs, knowing I was the sacrificial Jew who would soon be forced to follow the pope. That's one of the pitfalls of working open-mic nights as a beginner; when a more established comic pops in, he gets to go on next, regardless of the lineup. When it's Robin Williams, you might as well go home and announce your retirement. He was one of the most incredible stand-ups I have ever witnessed. His unprecedented way of riffing through a crowd with lightning-quick speed, spontaneity, and improvisation absolutely blew me away. I was in awe of how courageous and incredibly gifted he was to work that way without a net. He was equally astounding and unpredictable every time he graced a stage. There was no one like Robin at that time, nor is there anyone like him today.

Bill Cosby, Richard Pryor, Jay Leno, Rodney Danger-field, Steve Martin, Robert Klein, David Letterman, Richard Lewis, and Robin Williams were the monsters when I was starting out, and they set the bar so damn high that their level of excellence still holds strong. I'm honored to say that over the past thirty years, I have had the pleasure to meet or work with several of these idols, including Robin, who truly was one of the kindest and most humble guys in the business. I'm so grateful to have had the opportunity to work with him on *The Crazy Ones* and to have witnessed firsthand his brilliance and humanity.

Life has a way of throwing us those open-mic moments. They can be brutal to live through, but they are also some of the most important events in shaping our backbones, our courage, and our determination to succeed. After following Robin that night, I could have decided comedy wasn't for me, out of fear, insecurity, or plain common sense. But our passions choose us more often than we choose them, especially in the arts. We don't have a choice but to persevere.

Yes, this book is about letting some shit go in order to achieve happiness, *but* if you're bitten by something—a passion, a drive, an insatiable desire to stay awake during your colonoscopy—go for it, my friends. Reconnect with the aspirations you've squashed under twenty extra pounds of Cheez Whiz and shame, not that there's anything wrong with that. Your time may be yet to come. Remember, it ain't over until your children are fighting over who gets your presidential plate collection.

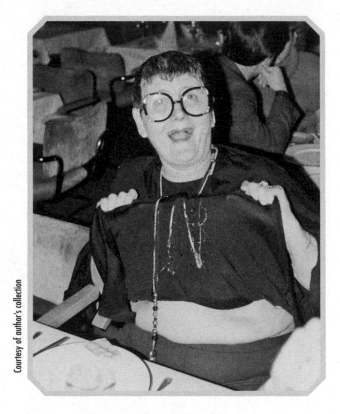

My first manager, Judy Thomas, 1984.

4

The Search for My Fifteen Minutes

I'm thirty-three years into this business, and I still feel my career can end at any minute. I'm not sure if that's just the mind of the fearful performer, or a midlife paranoia that leads me to believe that perhaps the bloom is off the rose and the Jamie Farr Dinner Theatre awaits my arrival. But if midlife is a time to reflect on one's career, I can say I am grateful to do what I love, particularly because at this point, it would be hard to transition into any other field. I often thought that if I hadn't gone into entertainment, I would have loved to be a child psychologist. Based on what you've read so far, I'm sure you'll agree that my roasting an eight-year-old and talking about scrotum rejuvenation for two hundred and fifty dollars an hour wouldn't go over very well.

I dropped out of UCLA after attending for only six weeks (don't act like you're surprised). My reasoning was: I couldn't figure out how taking Greek mythology was going to make me a better stand-up. Plus, my nightclub hours and college curriculum didn't mix. Honestly, I don't think I was college material. Everything moved too fast. Plus, I had just booked a national 7-Up commercial, and I was figuring (foolishly) that this was the beginning of my acting career and the spot would give me enough bank to cruise while I continued to work on my act. In other words, I had no idea what the fuck I was doing, especially since I had tried so desperately to get into UCLA. I wish I had stayed.

The 7-Up commercial that I was cast in needed six ethnically diverse actors to play a pickup basketball game in a schoolyard. After I passed the acting portion of the audition, they wanted to see how well we played basketball together. I was doomed. A half-court was set up behind the casting office, and I thought for sure I was screwed, until I devised a plan. I would be especially loud and energetic on the court, but as I ran around like a doofus, I would make sure I was never open, so I wouldn't have to prove that I could make a shot. This worked for about ten minutes until the director caught on and threw me the ball. I of course flinched and dropped it. The crew became so quiet "you could hear a mouse pissing on cotton in Georgia," as my comedian friend and early mentor Paul Mooney used to say. Why they hired me anyway is still a mystery, but let's just say you didn't see my Jew ass making any jump shots in the spot that aired. I was sitting on the bench, drinking a 7-Up, and cheering on my teammates. I guess I was just born to ride the pine.

After commissions and taxes, I blew through the remaining cash from the commercial in fourteen months, which led to my job as a waiter at the Pizza Cookery. For me, the best part about serving (which I did for four years) was that every table represented a new captive audience on whom I could try my material and impressions, the poor bastards.

It was around this time that my mom and Lionel came to me with some very exciting news. Lionel had just done the music for Jack Carter's son's bar mitzvah. Jack was a well-known, sharp, rapid-fire comic in his day, best known for working the Borscht Belt in the Catskills, along with opening for acts in Vegas and numerous television spots. His manager at the time was a large, boisterous, fearless woman named Judy "Trust Me" Thomas. Think Kathy Bates on steroids and ten times more butch. Her husband was the renowned British chef Derrick Thomas, who had his own restaurant at The Beverly Comstock Hotel in Beverly Hills. His patrons ranged from Paul McCartney to Johnny Carson.

My mom, who possessed a broad, grandiose persona as well, clicked immediately with Judy at the bar mitzvah and, upon hearing that she was an entertainment manager, hounded her for most of the evening until Judy agreed to meet her son "the amazing comedian." Two weeks later, I would meet the first person outside of my family to believe in me as a stand-up. With that belief would come a wonderful yet tumultuous ride, for Judy was a raging alcoholic who also housed a heart of gold.

Judy had a small, eclectic corral of ever changing clients, including an incredibly talented fifteen-year-old girl named Laura Dern who went on to become an Academy Award nominee. Marcia Wallace from *The Bob Newhart Show,* a promising kid named Perry Lang, a genius comedy/magic duo known as the Great Tomsoni & Co. (led by one of the world's greatest magicians, Johnny Thompson), Mary Martin (Peter Pan), Natalie Schafer (Mrs. Howell on *Gilligan's Island*), Russell Johnson (the Professor on *Gilligan's Island*), and several others would also come in and out of Judy Thomas Management. She had a small but potent reputation in the industry. She was bright, irreverent, and passionate, and when she believed in someone, you had better believe in that person as well.

Unfortunately, Judy was drunk every day by two P.M., but her incredible sense of humor and bravado kept most at bay as she carried out her business primarily from atop her enormous antique bed. She would lay sprawled out in sweats with a highball of bourbon in one hand and the phone in the other, donning her signature giant red-framed glasses. She had a true "old Hollywood" brilliance about her, though it was easily fogged by the daily bottle.

The day I met Judy, she had me do my act in its entirety in her living room. I was taken aback because stand-up comedy doesn't usually go over well in groups of one, but she "didn't give a shit." The more Judy drank, the more her sleepy eye went north. By the end of my mediocre fifteen-minute set, she appeared to have lapsed into a coma (I would later learn that this was around the time she would take her midday nap). Don't get me wrong, she did chuckle, sometimes politely, but I was ready to hear "Come back in ten years, when you know what you're doing." Instead, she poured another tipper, looked at me with those wonky eyes, and said, "You're cute, kid. Seven-foot Jew, don't play ball, that's funny shit. Keep the impressions. I know someone at the Bla-Bla Café on Ventura, but you're not quite ready yet, so I want you to play the living room until it's honed."

And that was the beginning of a twelve-year relationship that started with a year of me *literally* working my shit out in her living room. Anyone and everyone who would pop by would be asked to sit down for fifteen minutes of free comedy, from delivery people to the exterminator; Judy's husband, Derrick, who didn't laugh once in the first eight months; fellow agents or managers who would pop by to get paid on a loan or dope the racing form with her; her friend Sally Struthers, who let me hold her Emmy; or her friend Paul Mooney (he referred to Judy as the white Aunt Jemima). I also had to perform in front of the dog groomer; Judy's ninety-year-old mother, who was "communicating with aliens"; and, of course, Jack Carter. To Jack, I owe a great debt of gratitude: after seeing me work my stuff in front of Judy's gardener, he put his own reputation on the line and asked his buddy Norm Crosby to put me on his new show, *Norm Crosby's Comedy Shop*. That was where I made my national television debut in December 1981 at age twenty-one. The humbling part of it all was that I would watch my first television appearance from section thirteen at TGI Friday's in Woodland Hills, where I worked as a waiter. My national debut was sophomoric and ridiculously tame compared to what I do today. My watering days would last a bit longer.

Serving at TGI Friday's was a dream job for any budding comic. The Hollywood stereotype holds true, and with good reason; we all started as waiters, because there was always someone to sub in should an audition or gig come up. This was the pre-AIDS era, and the bar scene was crazy—Friday's took the term "meat market" to a new level. They were also known for introducing the Long Island Iced Tea and Loaded Potato Skins (smothered with cheese and bacon) to the world. You can imagine how stellar my diet was.

One night when I was working at Friday's, I waited on a gentleman who was dining alone. He ordered a nine-layer dip, which wouldn't be worth mentioning except that his serving had a piece of glass in it. He showed it to me, and after apologizing like Rodney Dangerfield, I brought over the manager, who comped his meal. As it turned out, the diner was one of the assistant managers at the Ice House, a comedy club in Pasadena where the greats like George Carlin, Steve Martin, and the Smothers Brothers used to work out their sets before hitting the talk show circuit. Naturally, I was dying for a spot. I was expecting that the glass incident would blacklist me for a while, but he booked me for an audition right then and there. This just proves what I've always said: you buy a Jew a meal, and magic happens.

I passed my audition and became a regular MC at the club, where I ended up working with their main booker, Elaine Tallas-Cardone. Believe it or not, that wonderful gal is now the comedy booker at my own comedy club in Vegas, thirty-two years later. The Ice House has retained its reputation as one of the greatest rooms in the country because of Bob Fisher, the owner, who is still a close friend of mine.

In 1983 Judy got a call from the manager of the Horn, one of L.A.'s oldest nightclubs, where I had just started performing. He inquired about my interest in auditioning for a new show called *Star Search,* to be hosted by Ed McMahon. Judy jumped on the opportunity, and a few days later, I found myself onstage at the Horn, during the day, auditioning in front of one guy. Just like in Judy's living room. He was the casting director for *Star Search,* and he looked like he was eighteen. His name was Steve Stark, and I credit that kind young man with giving me my break. This was the opportunity that would get my career rolling.

The following February I won the grand prize on *Star Search* and pocketed a hundred thousand dollars. When Ed McMahon announced my name as the grand champion in the comedy category, I saw Judy stand up in the audience in her drunken excitement, lift her sweater, and flash everyone in the Aquarius Theatre. She used to love showing off her giant boobs to the world. She was a very large woman, so I imagine she did this purely for shock value, but it was not the way I had wanted that night to end. The same can be said for my parents, who were seated in her row. This was not the first or last time Judy would embarrass me, but my loyalty and love for her, combined with a lack of belief in myself, made me stick it out for several more years. Still, it seemed that every time we made some headway, her drunken reputation or outbursts would bite us in the ass.

On one such occasion, Judy called the manager of the Improv comedy club on Melrose a cocksucker to his face on a packed Saturday night because my slot was bumped two times in a row (a common occurrence if you were a newbie). In hindsight, this was hysterical, but in reality, I wouldn't perform at the Improv for fifteen years after that night. Luckily, I already had my "home club," the Ice House. It was there that I would continue to work up the ranks and polish my chops.

Four weeks after winning *Star Search,* I would make my debut on *The Tonight Show*, thanks to Ed McMahon, at the ripe old age of twenty-three. To say being on that show for the first time as a young comic is surreal is a crude understatement. I remember standing offstage on the other side of the curtain I had grown up staring at, thinking, *What the fuck am I doing here?*

I heard Johnny start my intro right after the band trailed off from a commercial, and I thought I was going to lose it. But that's when you see what you're made of. As scared as I was, I knew I belonged. My set was decent; he gave me the coveted okay sign, and I walked off and couldn't remember a thing. I wasn't invited to the couch my first time on, but I knew I was strong enough to come back, and I did four months later.

Soon after my thirtieth birthday, I sat down with Judy and had a heart-to-heart talk. The topic was the same as it had been for years: her alcoholism. She had only two working clients left, and I loved her like a mother, but in my heart, I knew if I stayed much longer, I was going to go down with the ship. Things were finally rolling for me, and the dysfunctional cycle with Judy had to end. But I needed to try one more time to give her the opportunity to get well. I gave her an ultimatum: "Get help for the booze, I'll pay for the rehab. If you agree to this, I'll wait it out with you. If not, I have to leave." Judy was in total denial and acted like she had no idea what I was talking about. The following day I reiterated our conversation, of which she had no recollection. The day after that, I officially moved on.

I will always be indebted to Judy for her passion, instinct, and the love we had for each other. But my tendency to hang on too long to unhealthy relationships, business and personal, would become an obstacle for me throughout my adult life. As I have learned, there is sometimes a fine line between loyalty and self-sacrifice.

Judy would pass away eighteen months later from a massive heart attack, most likely attributed to her weight and acute alcohol poisoning. I received the news from our shared business manager as I waited at a Western Union at the Barbary Coast Hotel in Vegas to receive some cash for my gambling habit. Ironically, my own issues with booze were just around the corner.

The first review I ever received was when the winners of *Star Search* '84 performed for one night at Carnegie Hall in New York City. It goes without saying that none of us deserved to be on that stage at that point in our careers, but that didn't stop me from running down from my hotel room the following morning to the newspaper box. I remember standing on Fifty-sixth Street and Seventh Avenue, pulling *USA Today* from the rack, and reading the review. They referred to me as "instantly forgettable." I had to read the one-line review three times until it sank in. I even tried reading it with one eye closed, thinking it might be a little less painful. No such luck. Bottom line, I knew deep down they were right. After all, this was New York, undoubtedly the greatest city in the world, especially when it came to entertainment. They knew their shit.

Two things that have helped me greatly in my career are humility and self-awareness. The ability to know one's strengths and weaknesses and to successfully maneuver between the two is key in any occupation. But here's the catch: it takes a big-ass ego to hop onstage and much less of one to know when to get the fuck off. Part of the art is balancing the two. "Always leave 'em wanting more," as the old showbiz adage goes. It's no different in everyday life, though I wouldn't suggest using it as your strategy in the bedroom.

5

Early Road

I have to say that one of the best lessons I learned about fending for myself was when I went on the road for the first time, opening for the legendary, brash racial comic Paul Mooney. Paul was known for pushing the limits of race and shoving it back in the faces of white folks, and that was something wonderful to behold. He brought fearlessness to a whole new level, especially one week in 1982 at the Comedy Corner in Dallas, Texas.

After the show on closing night, the manager refused to hand over the exact amount that Mooney was contractually owed for the gig. The manager made it seem like the club hadn't made enough money that week, which, of course, was bullshit. Paul asked the manager to get the owner on the phone, and the guy refused. One thing led to another, and Paul and the manager found themselves outside the club where things began to escalate intensely. Mooney turned to me and said, "Remember this shit, Monster"—his pet name for me—"though you probably won't have to go through it, 'cause you're fucking white." I knew he was right and I hated that he was. Then he got right into the manager's face and said, "You either tell your scumbag boss to get over here with my money, in cash, or me and the Monster will burn this motherfucker to the ground!" We? What fucking "we"?

I was twenty-two and thought I was headed to jail. Ten minutes later, the owner of the club showed up in his pajamas and gave Mooney an envelope of cash. Paul made him count it, and it was accurate. He grabbed the dough, and we got into our rental car. Mooney said to me, "You drive," and proceeded to sit in the back as the white boy chauffeured. I'll never forget looking into the rearview mirror as Mooney said, "And that's how Jesse robbed another bank. Never let them fuck with you, Monster. Never."

I owe Paul a lot because he forced that club to use me as his opener when no one knew me. Several club dates followed, because Dallas was a hub for a lot of cats touring the country. And he taught me something I've never forgotten: as he used to tell everyone, "There's lots of stars, but only one Moon(ey)." No shit.

One of the craziest and funniest club comics I ever

worked with on the road was John Fox. His partying was as legendary as his act, and they usually took place simultaneously. He was a crusher onstage and had a reputation for closing every bar in town before moving on to the next city. John had this acerbic surfer-dude persona on- and offstage, and the gals just loved him. Sure, he aimed high with the ladies, but by two A.M. anyone was fair game for "Foxy."

Back in the early eighties, I opened for John in San Jose, California, at the Last Laugh, and after the show, we went out with a couple of ladies from the audience for some cocktails. My gal was a stone-cold five and worked at a veterinary clinic. Unfortunately, her job was starting to rub off on her face. John's gal was a solid six, a flight attendant who appeared to be hitting the free peanuts awfully hard. She had birthing hips without the kids, if you catch my drift.

John and I were pounding them back pretty good, but Fox could outdrink anyone. My gal slipped away after a couple margaritas, never to resurface, while John and his lady hopped into her car and disappeared. I took a cab back to the "comedy condo" to sleep it off.

It was around five A.M. when John stumbled back into the condo with no shoes, a torn shirt, and part of a rope in his back pocket. I witnessed this because in those days, the opening act slept on the couch. "What the fuck happened to you?" I asked.

"Not really sure, but I need to buy some shoes before showtime tomorrow," John slurred as he staggered into his bedroom. Later that night, he held court backstage, as he often did, and we got the skinny. Supposedly, John and the flight attendant got a little kinky, and since both were piss-drunk, it got a bit crazier than expected. The gal wanted to be tied up, and she conveniently had all the necessary items to fulfill her fetish.

John's story went something like this: "I ain't no fuckin' Boy Scout, so I'm trying to tie up this bitch the best I can, right? I got one leg tied to the footboard, arms tied to the posts on the headboard, the whole friggin' shebang. She's saying, 'Tighter, tighter!' and the whole room is spinning 'cause I'm so fucking drunk. She can't move, and her eyes are rolling back into her head like she's channeling. Just when I'm about to fly the friendly skies, she says, 'You have any more of that shit we did in the car?' I say yes, and then I notice I musta left it in her fucking car, because it ain't on me. She says, 'Grab my keys, go get it, and rush back up.' Shouldn't be that hard except for the fact that she lived in a gigantic apartment complex, one of those huge Oakwood rent-by-the-month shit-holes. Like a thousand apartments or something. Being that I was smashed when we got there, after leaving her apartment, I had no fuckin' idea where her car was and even less of an idea where her apartment was. So I never made it back."

Normally, Fox would have chalked that up to just another one-night stand gone wrong. But he tied her up a bit too well. The airline and her friends went looking for her after two days when she didn't show up for work. Rumor has it she was still tied to the bed but fine. Pissed, hungry, and soiled but fine. Which in actuality is how we all end up anyway. She got a little look into her future.

In the early eighties, I also got the chance to open for the brilliant comedian Kevin Nealon, before his reign on *Saturday Night Live*. We were working a five-night gig during the summer in Oklahoma City at a club in a mall called Jokers. We came straight from the airport in the morning and arrived together at the club to pick up the keys to the nearby condo where we would be staying. Nealon's picture was plastered all over the box office, yet when we met the girl working the ticket booth, she had no idea who we were. It was at times like this when Nealon's gift for improvising the absurd shone through. The dummy in the booth said, "Can I help you?"

Nealon replied, "Yes. We're here to fix the air-conditioning."

"Toasty as all get-out today, ain't it, boys?" and she started to let us in.

Nealon followed with "Where's your main thermostat, ma'am?"

"Believe over thar in Jimmy's office," said the inbred cashier.

"Terrific. Let's take a look-see, shall we? Ready, Donny?" Nealon threw to me.

"Yes, sir" was just about all I could get out because I was biting the inside of my cheek. The next thing I knew, Kevin was standing on someone's desk, taking out ceiling tiles and handing them down to me as he attempted to assess the situation. We started riffing back and forth, using bullshit air-conditioning terminology as the chick's eyes started to gloss over. I remember him asking her if she had a paper clip or stapler. As she began to look around, the owner of the club walked in and, upon recognizing Kevin as his head popped out from the ceiling, erupted into hysterics. It still took the gal a few more minutes to put it together, bless her heart. After all, we were in Oklahoma.

Although I am grateful to be at peace with middle age now that I've arrived, I am also glad to have experienced those wild times that can happen only in one's youth. Eventually, you reach a point in life where you'll shell out to rent a room at the Best Western before sleeping on someone's floor; where you can't stay out all night because your sciatica is working overtime; where you know that taking home the crazy loose broad with the harelip won't be worth it come morning, even though you haven't gotten laid since the last presidential election. But we must learn from experience, and let's face it: sometimes, the more fucked up the story, the better the memory.

I was nuts over him.
Get it? (with Sammy Davis Jr. at the Desert Inn, 1986)

6

Learning Las Vegas

Vegas represented everything I ever longed for: scantily clad women, booze, gambling, all-night dining, and the best showrooms in the world. What else does an unhealthy male need? Not to mention the decadent hotel suites. I once had a bidet that sat six for dinner. There's something about the town that to this day makes me say, "I shouldn't be doing this." They have hookers on billboards with phone numbers, for crying out loud! Make sure you get your shots, people.

There's a reason old folks flock to Vegas. Not just because the living is cheap, but because they know they're in their final round and figure maybe they'll finally hit that jackpot, or get in free to *Nudes on Ice* one last time. They think they're at the age when they've got nothing to lose, why not risk the insulin money?

Many of my most exciting and formative years as a stand-up comedian were when I worked as the opening act for some of the biggest headliners in the industry. Being an opener is not only good bread, it's also an invaluable opportunity for a comic to hone his craft. No one comes to see you, so when you do well, you know you've earned it. In my mid-twenties, I started working all the casino towns with the likes of Frank Sinatra, Sammy Davis Jr., Smokey Robinson, Liza Minnelli, Diana Ross, the Beach Boys, the Temptations, Julio Iglesias, the Righteous Brothers, and David Copperfield. After years of working with musical icons, I learned many important things, not the least of which was: if there's a rock-and-roll heaven, the pharmacy's jammed.

Specifially, one thing I learned as an opener was to do my job and then fade into the background, giving the star the privacy and space he or she needed and desired during the course of the engagement. If you were clingy, you were dead. If you were invited to hang out or go to dinner, it was a true honor; it meant you were "in" and that future employment was probable. On the other hand, if you bombed, you quickly got used to the hotel cafeteria.

The first headliner I opened for was Charo. That's right, you heard me. I admit it. It was at Harrah's in Reno, Nevada, and I'd be lying if I said I wasn't excited. My mother loved her and believed this was a fantastic opportunity. Me, I just wanted to see those tits up close—the ones that Merv Griffin never noticed all those years on his show. She had those wonderful Latina cans that reminded you to buy milk the moment you saw them. I can only assume she had areolas like dinner plates. The first time I met her, I slipped her a twenty and told her I needed more towels, pronto. She yelled, "Coochi-coochi," shook her blouse clowns, and we were off to the races.

Women have such a wonderful advantage in that they can make you forget all that is important with just a hint of cleavage. With Charo, there was no hinting. They were out like Ellen. If only men had the power to sexually overpower their surroundings using bodily innuendo. If only guys could leave the house before a date with just, I don't know . . . one testicle out. Maybe let them both out once in a while! Be free; teabag a midget if you feel like it. That's legal in Nevada, by the way.

The first headliner to bring me into Las Vegas, and the first artist I went on tour with, was Crystal Gayle. What she lacked in the Charo department, she made up for in hair. I opened for her at the Desert Inn in September 1986. She was a lovely lady with the voice of an angel and exquisite hair that flowed four inches from the floor. She made me weep. I used to have fantasies of wrapping her up in those long locks and then pull-starting her like an old Toro. I spent a couple months on the road with her and learned that country music people are in a class of their own when it comes to the wonderful way they treat their crew and fellow performers. I was scared to death on many a night, but Crystal and her people were so pleasant and encouraging that it made things much easier on me.

One night before one of our shows in Vegas, I got a call from the hotel operator saying that "Mr. Bill Cosby" was on the line for me. Now, you need to understand that the first comedy album I ever listened to, when I was nine, was Bill Cosby's *Why Is There Air?* I would have to sneak into my brother Jeff's room and play it on his hi-fi when he wasn't home. Cosby was a god, not only to me but to possibly every single stand-up who came after him.

I had a couple friends who were impersonators, so I immediately thought it was a buddy fucking with me. "Sure, put him through, please," I said.

"Hey, Brad, it's Bill Cosby. How they treating you over at the D.I.?" The voice was undeniable.

"Good. Thank you," I squeaked.

"Listen, I'm playing at the Hilton up the road, and I'm filling in as guest host for Carson tomorrow night. Thought you may want to do a spot on the show. We tape at four P.M. in Burbank and since we both have shows that same night, Carson is kind enough to send his jet."

There was no way this was real. I looked in a mirror next to the bed to see if I had died.

"Hello?" he said.

"Yes, please, thank you. Unbelievable, Mr. Cosby. What an amazing opportunity. Thank you."

"Great. My assistant will send all the info to the hotel, and I'll see you tomorrow afternoon on the jet." Click.

This would be my third appearance on *The Tonight Show*, and I wasn't sure what material to use. I was two weeks into my Vegas gig with Crystal and opening with jokes about the casinos; then I would work the crowd a bit and end the set every night with impressions. My Cosby impression always got a huge response, so I assumed that would kill on the show, especially with the Coz himself sitting behind the desk. But a *Tonight Show* set usually took at least four weeks to structure while trying it out at clubs. This was tomorrow. *Breathe, fucker.*

I slept about four hours that night and changed my outfit three times, like a bitch, before heading to the private terminal at McCarran Airport, where Cosby and Carson's Learjet awaited. It was my first time on a private plane, and as I made my way up the stairs, I felt my knees shaking. As I was boarding, I saw Cosby sitting on the eight-seater, facing the rear of the jet, reading a *USA Today*. His face was plastered on the front of the Entertainment section. Remember, this was 1986, and *The Cosby Show* was number one in the ratings. It was all too friggin' surreal for me to digest at that moment. I was trying not to think too much about this amazingly wonderful situation, while focusing on how grateful I was, as well as trying to contemplate what six minutes of material I was going to do on the show, and where the hell was I going to sit my big dumper down?

"Have a seat, Brad," Cosby said without turning around.

"Hey. Great. Thanks," I managed to say. I was frozen. *Where should I sit out of the seven remaining seats? If I sit in the row parallel to his on the opposite side of the jet, is that rude? Or do I allow him the space? Or should my seat be facing toward the tail, like his? Or is that too aloof, since I won't be looking at him?*

I must have looked like a fool, standing there with my head darting around like a chicken as I contemplated my seat. Cosby then picked up the *Los Angeles Times*, and sure as shit, a shot of him on the set of his show with the cast adorned the front of the Calendar section.

"Put it down there," Bill said as he pointed to the seat directly in front of him.

"Thought you'd never ask," I returned. His electric, signature downturned smile, with his eyes toward the ceiling and that slight shake of his head, broke the ice.

I plopped down across from the Coz and coiled my giraffe legs inward as much as possible, so as not to crowd him. It was quiet for twenty seconds (which felt like an hour), and then he looked up from his paper. We started to speak at the same time. He said, "Have some kiwi" as "Thanks so much for this opportunity" spilled from my yapper. His large finger pointed to a fruit and cheese tray we could never finish if there were ten of us.

"I'm good, thanks. I had an apple on the train," I said, trying to be funny. Nothing. Fuck me. I was bombing in front of the Master. The captain then popped his head out of the cockpit and said we should be in Van Nuys in about forty minutes.

"Lovely!" the Coz replied. "You ever been on one of these things?"

"I have not," I said, starting to breathe again.

"Smooooth," he said. "Have some Brie."

We started talking comedy and Vegas, and he told me how much the city had changed, how the glamour and class had left, how someone was wearing flip-flops during his show the other night at the Hilton. Everything he said had that keen Cosby observational slow pitch behind it. I wanted to laugh at everything because I just loved this man so much, but I never wanted to appear like a kiss-ass, so my nerves created an odd chuckle I'd never heard before. Luckily, he plowed through, then changed the subject: "I hear you do an impression of me."

Weird chuckle, again. "Yes, I do . . ."

"Yeah, don't do that tonight on the show," he said. "Just be yourself."

I was speechless. I was staring right at him. Was he fucking with me? My ass started to gnaw away at the seat cushion. Back then my impressions were the strongest part of my act. And to impersonate him *in front of him* on national television? What could be better than that?

Feeling desperate, I said, "People love when I do you, Mr. Cosby. You were one of my first impressions."

Oddly, he wasn't buying it. And I got the feeling he really meant what he said. "Have some melon," he replied as I considered jumping from the plane.

We arrived at NBC Studios in Burbank an hour before taping, and I was still having a hard time comprehending my own reality. I was entering the most famous soundstage on earth with the most famous comedian alive. Cosby was immediately swarmed by half a dozen bodies asking him what he needed and how they could be of assistance. I was shuffled off into a dressing room where I was told a segment producer would be popping by in a few minutes to go over my set. What set? I hadn't decided what I was doing yet. Since the Coz had emphatically suggested I not impersonate him, I was at a total fucking loss.

I looked at the crumpled piece of paper that had most of my act scribbled on it in bullet points. The jokes appeared alarmingly unfunny. I couldn't end with my other impressions because I had done them the last time I was on. *Okay, maybe the bit about the Iranian clerk at 7-Eleven?* I thought. *Shit, that's so hacky, and the Coz is pretty PC about stuff, so he could hate that.* I also used to do an impression of this incomprehensible black NBA player. It killed in the clubs, but he'd for sure leave on the plane without me if I did that one. I was close to calling my mommy.

Fifty minutes later, Cosby gave me a very nice introduction and I wandered out to a gracious crowd. I started with some bits and was doing okay, but nothing remarkable. I knew I needed to end strong, and my instincts told me there was only one way to go about it. It was my ass on national television, and I knew the Cosby impression would kill, so I just had to strap on a pair and do it. The audience went nuts for it. When I looked over to the Coz behind Johnny's desk, I could see he had his head down, reading the blue cards that would intro the next commercial. He had stopped watching. My heart sank down to my size-fifteen Florsheim loafers.

Backstage after the show, he said nothing to me. Silence on the car ride back to the airport. Zero conversation on the jet. Two separate limos met us on the tarmac on our return to Vegas. I shook his hand and genuinely thanked him before getting into my gold Desert Inn ride. He nodded and told me to take it easy, then sank into his black Hilton stretch. Part of me was devastated. But as wonderful as it would have been to receive Mr. Cosby's seal of approval, I didn't regret my decision to go ahead with the impression. The set had ended on a higher note than it would have if I'd gone against my instinct. Sometimes we just have to do what we have to do.

If you're taking notes, here's a good one: the key to anything in life is to be *fearless*. This doesn't mean you won't experience fear, just that you can't let it dominate you. Especially in entertainment. And always in comedy.

When I teach my sitcom acting class, I try to emphasize the Four F's, which stand for: Fearless Freedom Finds Funny. If you want to be remembered, you've got to stir the pot.

My years working with the Righteous Brothers at the Desert Inn, and later at the MGM Grand, were possibly the most enjoyable of all my opener gigs. We had an immediate and genuine friendship that has lasted to this day.

Bill Medley and Bobby Hatfield were two incredibly gifted singers from Orange County, California, who rocketed to stardom as teenagers. They created the original blue-eyed soul with mega-hits like "Soul and Inspiration," "You've Lost That Loving Feeling," and "Unchained Melody." They were class acts and staunch family men and so down-to-earth. Their support and belief in me helped me grow the most as a comic during the four years I spent opening for them. They gave me the freedom to experiment and try bits and work outside of the box. And their manager of almost fifty years, David Cohen, had my back as if I were one of the Brothers. I learned so much from these legends when it came to appreciation and rapport with an audience.

I was raised on the music of Frank Sinatra, Tony Bennett, Sammy Davis Jr., and the icons of Motown, so you can imagine what it was like for me to share a stage with some of these artists whom I idolized. Sammy Davis Jr., in particular, had a special place in my heart years before I opened for him. He was one of my parents' favorites as well, and before they divorced and my dad moved out, he gave me his favorite album, *Sammy Davis Jr. at the Cocoanut Grove*. It was the coolest album ever: a double set with an amazing shot of Sammy performing on the cover. The photograph was lit in black and blue hues, illuminating the profile of this true genius.

I remember sitting with my father on the floor of my bedroom, riveted as Sammy did a medley from *West Side Story,* then "Birth of the Blues," "Come Back to Me,"and his masterful "Once in a Lifetime." His songs always reminded me of my dad because they were about personal struggles and love, both won and lost. Sammy's impersonations were also perfect, and my pop would mimic him doing the voices, especially Humphrey Bogart. My dad's Bogie was killer. I'll never forget the audience on the recording howling with laughter at Sammy's banter, followed by awed silence as he went into his signature "What Kind of Fool Am I?" I held the album close to my chest and told my father, "I'm going to work with him one day," just to give him some hope in his world that seemed to be riddled with disappointment. He replied, "I bet you will." That promise became a reality twenty years later as my dad sat in his own booth in the theater at Harrah's in Reno.

Something that always fascinated me about Sammy was that when he went on the road, half of his house literally went with him. A mini-semi would follow his tour bus, loaded with dozens of tiny suits on wardrobe racks, paintings and photographs, a couple of his favorite recliners, and a cocktail-table-size Pac-Man game that he spent hours playing, competing with band members and backstage friends.

The only thing Sammy liked more than performing was performers. He was one of the most generous superstars ever. He would throw an opening-night party in every town he performed in, taking over either a local movie theater or the entire floor of a hotel. Several local performers would be invited; some he knew and others he would get to know. He was the consummate host and happy to make anyone feel at ease. He also had a killer sense of humor and, of course, that crazy, infectious laugh.

One of my favorite Sammy stories came from when we were backstage after a rehearsal at the Fox Theatre in Detroit. Some of the band members and I were hitting the soda machine. It was in the late eighties, before the machines took bills. The boys all had change except for me, and when Sammy walked by, I casually asked him if he could please change a twenty.

He looked at me with that infamous grin and, without missing a beat, replied, "Kid, a twenty *is* change." That was one of the greatest lines ever.

Sammy gave me one of the best perks as an opening-night gift. He sent me to the famous Chicken Ranch on his dime. His generosity gave me the pick of the litter. And her friend. Sadly, I was too nervous, too drunk, and too self-conscious to enjoy the full effect, and I was done so quickly that the broads felt obligated to give me a tour of the joint to show good faith. I was back in the limo so soon, the driver thought I was thrown out. This was a good example of "be careful what you wish for," because here I had twenty beautiful girls at my disposal, and my tendency was to make jokes and offhand remarks instead of making my choice and getting down to business. Even at twenty-seven, I was hiding behind my humor to break the ice, when there was not even any ice to break. They were ready! Half naked, lined up, and they probably just wanted me to shut the fuck up so they could get it over with and move on to the next john.

I wore protection, though I would have preferred to wear a wetsuit, I was so worried about catching something. What I did not anticipate was the inspection that the "lady" put my dick through. Before becoming a hooker, she must have worked for immigration at the Russian border. She tweaked my facile member into a garlic knot, looking for I don't know what. I asked if she was checking me for ticks. She mumbled something and then asked me several questions about a mole I had in my pelvic region. I countered with "You're the one fucking fifteen guys a night. When is it my turn to check out your tattered 'coin purse'?" So much for foreplay.

✧   ✧   ✧

I started opening for Julio Iglesias during his most popular period in America, following a duet he recorded with Willie Nelson entitled "To All the Girls I've Loved Before." Julio was an incredibly charming, great-looking, suave gentleman who loved the ladies almost as much as they loved him. His harem was ever changing and beautifully impressive. I would look on with envy as he wined and dined these beauties (most of whom were half his age) in his four-bedroom suite while I stood in line at the employee cafeteria at Caesars Palace.

He flew around the world in his private jet and had a palatial estate in Florida. His life was everything that every man prayed for, and it was happening to him as he approached middle age. I have a strong feeling he wasn't concerned about the dropping of his balls, and trust me, if it had happened, there would have been a solid ten waiting to catch them. I prayed that just once he'd throw me a gal he was tired of shagging. No such luck. None of them spoke English, either. I heard a French model pass me after a show once and whisper to her friend, "Stupit clown." If I had been a mime, she would have been mine.

Julio was selling out huge venues; we did a sold-out two-week stint at Radio City Music Hall in New York. It was an amazing experience except for one small detail: like his ladies, the majority of his audiences did not speak English. Unfortunately, nobody mentioned that to me in advance.

About two weeks into the gig, when very little of my material was working onstage, I asked Danny, the sound engineer who was at the board every night, if he had any suggestions. He suggested learning my act in Portuguese, Italian, or Spanish. Maybe French. All the languages Julio sang in during his concerts. I asked Danny, "If his audiences don't speak English, why the hell does he use a comic to open?"

"He likes to laugh before a show," Danny said. "He howled at Roseanne Barr when she opened for us."

"Great!" I said. "Get that bitch back. If not, maybe he can come out to the front of the house when I'm on and run around laughing. Make it sound like a crowd." Thank goodness for Danny. At least he got me. Once in a while I could hear his raspy chuckle coming from the board (a good indication of how quiet the audience was).

My favorite times on tour with any act were those hanging out with the band and crew. After all, I was one of them. One night, following a really strong set in front of Julio in Jones Beach, New York, I decided to celebrate with some tequila. Those were the days when Jose Cuervo Gold 1400 was my juice of choice. All I could find on the tour bus was some silver tequila, which was not user-friendly, but that didn't stop me from polishing off most of the bottle. When the double-decker tour bus pulled up to the hotel in Jersey a couple hours later, I forgot I was on the upper deck and proceeded to exit the bus by falling down and out, landing right on my face. Not the best way to exit. I woke up on the pavement with Julio's drummer, Dave, looking over me. He was a part-time fireman in his hometown and a great guy, and he suggested I go to the hospital. He also suggested I might have a serious drinking problem. I was in complete denial, though I did agree to go to the hospital. The emergency room was packed, and after staying an hour without being seen, I left with a fractured nose and two black eyes.

The next night I opened the show with "Take it from me, do *not* call Julio a Mexican. He does not like that. He's Spanish. Which I believe is a Mexican who gets laid a lot. Never really knew there was a difference." Then, pointing to my face: "Now I know." This was a New York crowd, and they ate it up. It was one of my best sets on the tour.

Four years ago I was given the opportunity to open my own comedy club in Las Vegas at the MGM Grand Hotel & Casino, returning to my roots in the town that helped get me started thirty years earlier. Even after all this time, I still get excited by the energy and possibility that is unique to Vegas. I think it comes from so much *wrong* being condensed into such a small amount of space.

If you need a vacation to kick-start the "new you" after reading this book, Vegas is the place to go. The wonderful part is that anything goes in this town, and if you're worried about coming off bad, too drunk, or inappropriate, the guy sitting next to you probably has you beat, so no worries. You can fill your piehole at twenty-four-hour buffets, lose your children's inheritance on a whim (they need to get off their asses and work anyway), get a happy ending from a tranny you didn't think was a tranny, burn yourself to a crisp taking a ten-minute nap by the lazy river by the pool (also known as the "freeway of urine"), hit another two buffets just because you have the coupons, then be the proudly sketchy "old person" at a nightclub where you can use all those dance moves you haven't broken out since prom. And when you fall into bed, happier than you've ever been, here's the good news: the next day, you can do it all over again.

Backstage at Bally's Las Vegas, 1989.

7

Perfectly Frank

It's difficult to talk longingly about yesteryear without sounding like an old fart. I never thought I would be the middle-aged guy saying, "Girls never dressed like that when I was in high school!" or "That's not music!" or "They don't make microwave ovens like they used to!" I never wanted to be that guy. Unfortunately, it's inevitable, because my laments about the differences from one generation to the next are valid.

My dad was "that guy" when I was growing up, and so was his father. Things are spiraling more out of control as a whole. Elvis shook his hips in skintight pants, and Bible-beaters thought it was the beginning of the end; today Drake is singing that his "dick is so hard it's making the metal detector go off," and even I've got it on my iPod. I'm not sure why. Maybe to signal to my teenage kids that I'm not as old on the inside as I look and feel on the outside. Or maybe it's because Drake is the only half-Jewish rapper.

Before my girlfriend, IsaBeall, and I started dating, I sent her two Sinatra songs on an iPod that I wanted her to listen to. They were two of my favorite songs of all time, "One for My Baby" and "The Way You Look Tonight." As it turned out, she already had both on her iPod. It was a Fisher-Price iPod, but who's judging? The fact that she was so much younger but had an appreciation for Sinatra made me optimistic. Maybe this middle-age dweller had something in common with this beautiful, bright, and exciting gal from the Northeast. In all honesty, like most things, it was pure attraction in the beginning. But it wasn't long until her golden heart and old soul broadsided me like the backhand of a pimp.

Sinatra and Sammy were close friends, and they shared a lot of the same reps. When I was opening for Sammy in Lake Tahoe, some of Frank's "boys" caught my act, and I was asked to open for Sinatra on New Year's Eve 1989 at Bally's in Vegas. I will never forget that phone call from my agent at the William Morris Agency, checking my availability. I was blown away that my agent actually had my number.

I drove from L.A. to Vegas on December 29, arriving at

Bally's at two-thirty A.M. As I drove down the Strip and approached the hotel, there it was: the marquee that would for the first time make me feel like I had arrived:

FRANK SINATRA

with Brad Garrett

Below my name, it read FREE SHRIMP COCKTAIL in letters twice the size of mine. That was Vegas. They knew the free shrimp would bring in more folks than Brad Garrett, so they were smart enough to roll with it.

The next issue was: how would I go over with Sinatra's crowd? These people had come from all over the world to ring in the New Year with the Legend. How could I get "roasty" with the front row if they were diplomats, stars, and notables wondering who the hell I was? But I had just bought a charcoal-gray tux from Charmer's Big 'n' Tall with a turquoise cummerbund and matching clip-on bowtie. In my pea brain, I felt ready.

I had learned early on that to make a splash as an opening act, you had to do stuff a lot of the other guys weren't doing, as in schlepping out and doing twenty minutes of observational material to the back wall. As far as the crowd was concerned, you were the time buffer in case the wife was running late or traffic sucked. They were not there to see you, and the sooner you understood that, the sooner you could get down to business.

At nine-thirty P.M. on New Year's Eve, Gino, Sinatra's road manager, came to me and introduced himself. He was pretty much what you'd expect: a congenial, no-nonsense goombah from Brooklyn with hands like canned hams and a slight waddle from either a holster or knee injury. I wasn't going to ask. He was inviting and to the point. He said, "We're holding ten. His jet was a touch late leaving the Springs." I nodded like an idiot. What did I know?

The forty-piece orchestra started to assemble. "Why are they setting up now?" I asked, thinking they had forgotten that I was going on.

Gino looked at me quizzically. "To play you on, schmuck."

I paced around backstage as I looked at some notes, too nervous to sit down or hang out in the nice dressing room that had been set up for me. I owed that courtesy, and the majority of my career in Vegas, to Richard Sturm, the president of entertainment at Bally's at the time. Minutes later, backstage got oddly quiet. I saw a man being whisked in through the doors, flanked by other very large men who made me look petite. Then I heard the whisper of a man's voice that was undeniable. It was Francis Albert himself. Afraid to look at him or even move, I stood in the wings and prayed to blend in as I tried to get a glimpse of the front row. That was when I heard Sinatra grumble, "Where's Dreesen?"

Jilly, his best friend and main confidant, responded, "Remember, Frank, he's opening for Glen Campbell tonight."

"No one told me," he said. The crew looked at each other,

knowing full well that this information had in fact been given to "Mr. S.," as all information always was. He added, "Why the hell would you hire someone to open who I've never seen before? And on New Year's Eve?" I felt a bead of sweat that smelled like vodka roll off my brow and into the corner of my very dry mouth. My ears tried to leave my body. My penis retreated into the darkest part of my zoobag.

"We saw him with Smokey [Sammy]. He does good," Gino added. Frank walked off.

In those early days, I usually had a couple drinks before a show, but on this night I didn't want anything to blame if I wasn't on target. After hearing that conversation, I wished I hadn't made the responsible choice. I was sober except for a mild hangover from the night before, where I had lost eighteen hundred dollars in roulette after downing about twelve shots of Rumple Minze (hundred-proof schnapps). That was a big hit to take for an opening act, especially considering I had 25 percent in commissions coming off the top of my wage. As my dad used to constantly explain to me, "If you want to blow two thousand gambling, you'll need to make about thirty-eight hundred in order to do so." My father always tried to drill into my head the difference between what I made and what I brought home after everyone dipped their beaks. In other words, I worked for free those three nights. But I was in Vegas opening for Frank, so who cared, right?

As Frank Sinatra Jr. slunk by me to conduct the orchestra, I asked Gino, "How long do I do out there?"

"I don't know. Ten, twenty. You'll know," he said.

I blanched. "What do you mean? How will I know?"

"I'm not following," said Gino.

"Well, with all due respect, there's a big difference when a comic is supposed to do ten minutes as opposed to twenty, because my opening bit depends on—"

"Whataya worried about? Have fun." Gino snorted. "It's New Year's Eve, for fuck's sake."

"Thank you. It's just—"

"When Frank's ready, we'll let you know. Simple." Again my idiot nod.

Just then the most amazing orchestra I had ever heard started to play a medley of Frank's iconic hits. I had a vomit burp and loosened my fifteen-dollar cummerbund. Some turquoise glitter got on my thumb. It was a six-minute musical prologue that ended with "The Summer Wind" and a drumroll that I felt in my anal cavity. Then the announcement: "Ladies and gentlemen, happy New Year and welcome to Bally's Las Vegas, where we are honored to present Mr. Frank Sinatra! A Man and His Music!" The applause and screams were so fucking loud it was as if the walls were going to come down. So loud that "But first . . . please welcome Brad Garrett" was impossible for the audience to hear.

Unfortunately, I heard it. Did he really just say "But first"? Are you kidding me? Was the announcer insane? "But first"? He should have said, "But instead of the person you *really* want to see, please bear with us as we kill some time with Brad Garrett!"

I took the stage to a smattering of light applause. The front row looked like a lineup in Jersey. Feeling the need to shake these folks up a bit, I said exactly that to them. As if that weren't enough, "Raise your hand if you've recently been indicted, and keep 'em there so I can see if you decide to reach for something" followed. Small titters started to build.

I actually heard a guy in the front say, "The balls on dis fuckin' guy."

Then his buddy next to him, "Where's Dreesen?"

I immediately went into some hacky casino material, followed by my Sammy Davis Jr. impression. By now I pretty much had the crowd's attention, and as people came in late, I took aim at them, going so far as to ask the lighting tech to put the spotlight on the stragglers. He obliged, to the crowd's delight. This was something that most openers wouldn't pull, so it got more attention than not. I quickly started to realize that most crowds love it when you break their balls. Especially the Sinatra cronies. Again, I needed to be fearless to get through it. I knew no other way.

Two guys with no necks slithered into the front row. I figured "fuck it" and went with "Maybe after the show, I can help you fellas drive the dead hooker out to the desert?" Some big laughs were starting to roll from the back of the cavernous room, and the front row loosened up a touch but remained rather chatty. It was Vegas on New Year's Eve, so they had been drinking since three P.M. I went back to the tamer material for a few minutes.

I've never had much structure when it comes to my act. Most of my set at that time revolved around being a seven-foot Jew, my smallish pecker, my parents' multiple marriages, and more ethnic stuff, which they ate up. Then I glanced into the wings and saw Frank and Gino standing there. I was twenty-two minutes in, and Gino gave me the "wrap it up" hand signal. I was off in sixty seconds to decent applause. As I walked past Mr. Sinatra, he whispered, "Wait here, you'll come out for a bow."

All the tension from needing to be well received, having to overcome Frank's obvious disappointment about not having his regular opener, and now the acceptance from the biggest man in show business was overwhelming. My three-hundred-dollar tux was drenched with flopsweat as I waited again in the wings.

Frank walked out, and as expected, the place went berserk. He grabbed his Jack Daniel's on the rocks from the piano, toasted the crowd in Italian, and smiled through what seemed like a five-minute standing ovation. "Welcome to Bally's, you gamblin' bums. Let's bring this New Year in right, okay?" More screams. "But first . . ." (not kidding) "How about a hand for the big guy who opened the show tonight." I couldn't believe this was happening. Nor could the audience. They thought they had gotten rid of me. "Come out and take a bow! Greg Barrett, ladies and gentlemen. Marvelous stuff. Greg Barrett!" And there I stood. Taking a bow to mild applause and someone else's name. With the greatest singer of all time standing right next to me. Shrimp cocktail would have been envious.

He called me Greg Barrett at least a dozen more times over the next four years. And I continued to bow to it. Because everyone knows you don't correct Frank.

A month after my stint with Sinatra in Vegas, I received a call to open for him in his home state of New Jersey at the Sands in Atlantic City. I had played A.C. several times in the past, and the crowds were a lot less predictable than those in Vegas, but I wasn't nearly as nervous as I had been on New Year's Eve. Besides, the fact that "Mr. S." wanted me back really boosted my confidence, as well as my credibility as an opening act.

I got into Atlantic City two days before the gig, because life was good and my hobbies had become drinking and gambling at warp speed. Because of my size, I had the capacity to handle what was becoming close to a fifth of nectar on any given night. I was a high-functioning alcoholic, and if you weren't one of the guys from the band or crew with me at three A.M., you wouldn't suspect I had an issue with the bottle. I was always pretty crazy and outlandish anyway.

I could do my job half in the bag and usually crush it as an opener, because all you really needed was a strong twenty-five minutes. The great thing about being a stand-up with a booze problem was that you had more than enough hours to sober up; you worked only thirty minutes a night. That said, many times the hours leading up to the show could be brutal when the nerves got the best of you, which was often.

Ironically, on that particular night in Atlantic City, the crowd was even more unruly than they had been on New Year's Eve in Vegas. There was a fight in the audience over seats moments before I was scheduled to go on. No one was thrown out; let's face it, who's going to tell these guys to leave?

I hit the stage right at nine and might as well have been invisible. There was a couple so drunk in the front row that they got up and started slow-dancing during my act as the guy sang "The Lady Is a Tramp" to his date. That's something that stays with you forever. The guy was in a top hat and tails, holding a cane and wearing dark shades. I called him "Mr. Peanut." His lady had a scary perm that shot out in all directions. "Next time," I told her, "tease your hair. Don't piss it off." The folks around them were not laughing, but the rest of the audience and the orchestra behind the curtain howled.

Next I went into a lame bit where I did impressions of Sammy playing blackjack with Carroll O'Connor and Jim Ignatowski from *Taxi*. Swear to God. Gino was laughing from the wings. By this time, he was very supportive of me and had become a bit of a drinking buddy. Just then from the audience, a large fella with no neck yelled, "Where's Frank?"

That caused another inquiry: "Where's the comic?"

A woman in a mink stole yelled, "Frankie! I love you!" Now the crowd was getting bigger laughs than I was. I wanted to die. And I got my wish. But before leaving, I did one ad-lib just for me, something comics sometimes do to amuse themselves, especially when things aren't going well.

I said, "You've been very . . . lifelike. Thank you. And stick around for Frank!" As I passed "Mr. S." in the wings, he whispered to Gino, "Find out what that means." The orchestra tried not to laugh, but they got it. It was a harmless inside joke. But some of the crew didn't agree.

As I sat in my dressing room, wringing the sweat out of my jacket and pouring four fingers of straight vodka, there came a knock at the door. It was Jilly and an enormous guy named Mike who wore an eye patch. "Hey, guys. Come in, please," I said.

"How'd it go out there tonight, Brad?" Jilly asked.

"Tight. Probably not the best night to record the album," I said with a chuckle. Stares. Then I countered to Mike, "I loved you in *Pirates of Penzance*." Now it was really quiet.

"Well, you're doing a fine job," Jilly said.

"Thank you. Appreciate it."

"One question, though. What did you mean when you said, 'Stick around for Frank'?"

"Oh, that? That was a silly joke. It meant nothing."

"Well, it musta meant somethin'. It was the last thing you said, right?" Jilly questioned.

"Correct" fell from my mouth. More uncomfortable bewilderment from guys I pictured dismembering me in my sleep.

"But they're here to *see* Frank," Jilly said.

"Exactly. Of course. And therein lies the joke," I stammered. "Stick around for Frank!" I tried again.

"I don't get it."

"Neither do I."

"I was making fun of myself. 'Stick around for Frank!' You know? He's comin' out!" Still nothing.

"But they're already here. Where are they going? They came to see Frank. Why do they need to stick around for him?"

"And *that's* why it's funny! They don't!" I pleaded as I prayed for a sudden stroke. They weren't getting it. It wouldn't go away. The room was getting smaller.

"Were you making fun that Frank is sometimes late to a show, like 'Stick around for Frank,' as in 'He'll be here soon, don't leave' kind of thing?"

"Lord, no. That is not my style, Jilly," I said. Though, of course, it was.

Just then Jilly looked to Mike, the sleeping mountain, and asked him, "What did you hear, Mike?"

And in broken human, he replied, "I thought I heard 'Stick it to Frank.'"

Now I was envisioning being crammed into the trunk of a Lincoln. "Wha? No! Never would I say 'Stick it to Frank'!"

Jilly held up his giant mitt. "Let's just forget it."

"Done. Thank you. Forgotten."

"Okay, good. 'Mr. S.' invited you for Chinese after the show. Small group. Downstairs. You know where I mean?" I did. And it was wonderful. I dined with a king and his court, and the jester ate his Kung Pao pork and didn't say a fuckin' word for the rest of the night.

By the way, turns out "Mr. Peanut" was John Gotti. Apparently, I have nine lives.

Tom Caltabiano

The cast of *Everybody Loves Raymond* shooting
the "Sweet Charity" episode in season 7.

8

The Road to Raymond

The early nineties was the time when things started turning for me. I was in my thirties and enjoying my decadent and fruitful prime. Unlike now, when I find myself primed for flesh-eating diseases and incontinence.

It was 1995, and I had just finished filming an episode of *Seinfeld* where I portrayed an auto mechanic, Tony, who stole Jerry's Saab because he wasn't giving the car the care it needed. I had seen him perform at a club in New York ten years prior, and even then I knew it was only a matter of time until he became a major star. I recently saw Jerry perform again, this time at a benefit in L.A., and pound for pound, he's still the most brilliant comic out there. He also appears to be the least tortured comic I have ever encountered. It's well known that his childhood was pretty normal, and I can't pick up any Jew-neurosis whatsoever. It worries me. How can one be that gifted without the dysfunction that plagues most performers? Maybe he's a Martian. Or a spy for the gentiles.

A couple of weeks before my *Seinfeld* episode aired, I was gaining a little heat in the television arena, and my managers got their hands on a CBS pilot script called *Everybody Loves Raymond*. I wasn't remotely on the network's radar, but my reps at the time used the recent *Seinfeld* gig to open the eyes of the executives at CBS. To this day, it remains one of the funniest pilots I have ever read. I heard that they were interested in possibly going out to some comics to play the role of Robert, Ray Romano's older brother, and the rumor was that the network was eyeing a very funny comic named John Mendoza for the part.

Ironically, with all my years on the comedy circuit, I had never met Ray. I knew of him as a really solid and talented stand-up, but our paths had never crossed. From the minute I read the script, I had an innate sense of who Robert was. I knew my interpretation of the character was different from what they originally sought, and I was told that "physically," I was at the other end of the spectrum as far as what they were looking for. Ray's real-life cop brother, Richard, on whom the character was based, was shorter and scrappier than Ray, very much unlike my oafish self. But for some strange reason, I just knew how to play Robert as I prepared for my audition. I knew I could downplay my size by keeping Robbie succumbed to the fact that he would always come in second in life's race with Ray. A lot of it would come down to how I carried myself in the role. As an actor, I had a secret when it came to playing him: I went in with the mind-set that Ray was an only child, they just forgot to tell Robert.

I auditioned several days later in front of Phil Rosenthal (who created the show along with Ray), Leslie Moonves, the president of CBS, Stu Smiley from HBO, and Lisa Miller-Katz, the casting director. This was the only audition Ray was not a part of because he was en route from New York at the time. As I began the audition, a slightly different, lower voice than my own emerged. It was the voice of a beaten man that you automatically cared about and rooted for as he dangled from the ledge of life. Phil was a great laugher and helped get the roll in the room started. I was asked to come back the following day, and the rest is history. Robert became the first supporting role to be cast.

A few weeks later, I met Raymond and promptly felt that we were doomed. How could this guy lead a show? He looked like the teenager you would see at Whole Foods spraying down the produce. With a demeanor like that of a kid who'd just witnessed his puppy being stolen and a profile taken from an Indian nickel, he was subdued and egoless, which I misdiagnosed as someone who should be on suicide watch. He had a nasal quality to his voice that I prayed was

seasonal. And he took hypochondria to a new level, request-
ing that different crew members weigh in on a "suspicious"
mole or confirm whether he was "the only one who smelled
propane" during rehearsal. I had never felt so omnipotent
around anyone in my life.

I remember asking Ray if he had ever done any acting.
He replied, "I was just fired from *NewsRadio*." I wanted to
flee like a hooker in church. How could this guy be so com-
pletely unnatural, lovable, and real all at the same time? And
then my T. Rex brain put it together: he was fuckin' perfect.
This was exactly who Raymond needed to be. And lucky for
us, he had a shitload of talent as a writer, as well as the acting
chops to play himself authentically. He was truly the every-
man whom a nation would soon fall in love with.

I remember how excited I was when I heard that the
great Peter Boyle had signed on to play our dad. That was
a big coup for the show, and we were all pumped to work
with him. Ray was a little intimidated by Peter at first, but
then again, he was also intimidated by one of the three-year-
old twins, who I felt all along were circus midgets. I guess I
shouldn't use the word "midget." Out of respect, let's use the
term "ground angels." Peter was one of the sweetest guys
in the world, so our comfort was established early on, along
with our adoration.

Peter was a true individual, the same affable person to
everyone, and had zero airs. He did things his way and at
his tempo. He ate what he wanted, went to the gym if he

felt like it, and said what was on his mind. He didn't buy the hype or expectations that went along with aging or Hollywood. He was bald at twenty-three and wouldn't be caught dead wearing a toupee unless it was for a gag. He was adept at playing both comedy and drama and was married to a writer from *Rolling Stone*. John Lennon was the best man at his wedding, for God's sake! He was all man. Almost to the point of killing the cast.

You see . . . Peter, unfortunately, had a flatulence problem. He gave farts a bad name. But in the beginning, it was one of the biggest mysteries to ever hit the *Raymond* set, because no one knew where these deathly, silent scuds were originating from. Let's be honest, any time a fart creeps into a room, everyone automatically assumes it's the big guy. People figure that the giant's colon is at capacity and withering under immense girth and constant discomfort. I felt Romano glaring at me like "Why don't you just fess up, Garrett, and admit you ate the gumbo, so we can all move on." But that was not the case. And these fumes would haunt Stage 5 at Warner Bros. up until season four on a particular night in early spring.

We were filming an episode in front of the studio audience, and one of the cameras went down prior to a scene when the cast was supposed to enter through Ray and Debra's kitchen door, all in a heated argument. Rosenthal yelled his infamous "Hold!" as a cameraman tried to fix the B-camera. So there we were: Ray, Patty, Peter, Doris, and I huddled together in a four-by-four-foot area just off the set, awaiting our entrance. And there it came. Like an invisible gut-wrenching fog from a buffalo's brown star. And there was nowhere to go. Ray closed his mouth and opted to breathe through his nose. This used up 50 percent of the available air. Doris's makeup started to run. One of Patty's new breasts began to deflate. My hair gel ran into my eyes. And that was when we heard Peter meekly say, "Sorry." Yet the most amazing thing is what he said next: "But I gotta tell ya . . . I got two more comin'." That's when you know you have a real ass problem—when you can actually tell how many are left in the chamber. I never wanted to hear the word "Action!" more in my life. And so it was that the Phantom Farter was finally revealed. And just like global warming and homely strippers, it was something we all had to learn to live with.

Doris Roberts, who played Marie, was the only cast member who could outdrink me. The broad could party and loved to play cards. It was like we were separated at birth, right down to the forty-two-inch waist. The woman is a tenacious self-promoter and will go to a ribbon cutting at the Pottery Barn if there's free champagne. We were never sure how old she was, but when we were all traveling to film an episode in Italy, I noticed she had a luggage tag with a picture of the *Titanic*. She's an extremely gifted actor, and you can't imagine anyone else playing the role of Marie.

I felt Patty Heaton was the anchor to the show as far as

being able to play Ray's wife, Debra, with strength and forti-
tude, as opposed to the stereotypical sitcom wife who plays
the powerless victim. On the show, she was surrounded by
this band of crazies, and she would fight against the powers of evil hilariously. Even before the new boobs, she had
a sorority swagger about her that few midwestern women
possess, and I always found that very sexy. She reminded me
of this chick in high school who turned me down for a date
because I was a Jew. I found that very titillating. If I had my
way, Robert and Debra would have been caught banging in
the final episode. Don't judge me, I'm allowed to dream.
But Patty being a Republican made it easier for me to emotionally move on.

Robert's girlfriend and eventual wife, Amy, was played
by Monica Horan. For those of you who are unaware, she
was (and is) the real-life wife of our faithful showrunner,
Phil Rosenthal. So rest assured, she got the job by doing
something no other actress would do: fuck Phil. (I believe
that was also a Tarantino movie.) It was so much fun playing opposite Monica. I used to love that surprised look she
would get on her face during filming. It was as if she'd found
a lucky penny during her gyno exam.

In the nine years I worked on *Raymond,* we had a lot of
laughs, and as cliché as it may sound, we really were like a
family. We were surrounded by brilliant writers and a commitment to do the best work that we could. I was one lucky
bastard to be allowed on that bus.

Now, on the rare occasions when Ray and I get together to do a stand-up tour, golf, or play poker, we compare ailments and the amount of stiffness we feel in the morning. Unfortunately, that stiffness is in the wrong area. Both in our fifties now, we find ourselves bombarded with thoughts of what will truly lie on the other side of this hill. He's a lot richer than I am, so at least he can buy the cure for most anything or purchase the moon if Earth gets too crowded. Me? I'm gonna keep up with the Icy Hot, hide that quick-dissolving aspirin next to the alarm clock, and pray the hip gives out before the ticker.

9

Goodbye, Sauce

Sammy Davis Jr. used to quote two great lines about boozing. One was: "If I knew I was going to live this long, I would have taken much better care of myself." The other he coined after quitting the juice: "It's difficult to wake up in the morning and realize this is the best I'm going to feel all day."

After the first season of *Raymond* wrapped, I took a job in a horrible independent film where I portrayed a demented and homicidal postal worker. They should have cast the director. Up until that point, I had worked very little in film and thought it could be a move in the right direction for my career. Almost every naive actor at one point or another thinks, *This could be the one*. After just a couple days on the set, I realized I wouldn't have to worry about the film ever seeing the light of day. I recall one scene where my character was sitting in the bathroom eating SPAM out of a can as his nose bled into the gruel and he continued to eat it. Film noir at its best.

After the film wrapped, I headed off to Hawaii with a lovely gal I had met on the project who happened to be clean and sober and often spoke at A.A. meetings. Now I hear she goes around the country "channeling voices of wisdom from ancient prophets" to add dimension and clarity to strangers' lives for a nominal fee, DVD included. It pains me to say this, but some people are just better off drinking.

We weren't a great match for a variety of reasons, not the least of which was my excessive alcohol consumption. I recall hitting the minibar at the hotel pretty hard as she was taking a bath, thinking I was being discreet, as if she didn't already know I was an alkie.

On my third day in Maui, I read in *Variety* that *Raymond* had been picked up for a second season. Les Moonves, the president of CBS and one of the most ballsy and creative minds in television broadcasting, believed in the show enough to move it to the plush timeslot after *Cosby* on Mondays (we had been floundering on Friday nights). Later that evening I found myself at the Hula Bar, pounding down one after another as I sat alone, celebrating the news that after twenty years of canceled shows and the brutal club circuit, I might actually be on a hit. Or at least have a job for a while without living out of a suitcase.

There was a Hawaiian trio playing thirty feet away from me, and I remember thinking, *I drink when the news is bad and drink when the news is good. This shit's eventually gonna kill me.* I hit an emotional bottom. Fortunately, it wasn't as devastating as it could have been, but I had started to black out from heavier nights of drinking, and this worried me greatly. What if one night I never woke up, like Judy? I was living a life perpetuated by fear, and it just wasn't me. How could I be so fearless onstage and so petrified in real life? My daily reality wasn't consistent with who I was deep down, and it was all because I was hooked on the sauce.

The biggest fear of any working performer struggling with sobriety is: "Will I be as good straight?" It doesn't matter if it's a singer, comic, actor, writer, director, dancer, bricklayer, or painter. Any artist who has had success while high fearfully asks this question, and with good reason. Many of us have that dark hole in our being to contend with, and what we decide to fill it with is up to us. Many times we take out one ingredient only to fill it with another. We tackle the alcohol but are often left with the "ism." Artists in general tend to be complicated beings with conflicting voices going on in their heads. And you better believe, substances have their own voices. They try to woo you into needing them and not leaving them, which fits right into the void left by your guilt, doubt, and low self-esteem. They can also promise to give you the high you get from performing; it's an experience that can be so wonderfully intense, you may find yourself tempted in your downtime to try and artificially re-create what you felt onstage.

The other unfortunate trait of the artist's mind is that it's almost never allowed to turn off. True art is forever evolving and questioning, and once you delve into booze or drugs that appear to tame the brain into checking out, you find an artificial peace. In reality, you've just made the brain work overtime (along with the rest of the body), because as we know, the substances take a hell of a lot more work to filter out than do without. But I would be a liar if I told you that checking out did not fill a needful gap at times in all those insecure, stressful years, even though it came with a high price in the long run.

Now, on that particular night at the Hula Bar, I happened to take notice of what appeared to me to be a "perfect family." The father was the kind of guy I always wanted to look like, and the wife was the kind of woman I felt I would never have. But it was something about their two kids that moved me the most. My whole life, I had always dreamed of being a father. I wanted to have the same kind of relationship with kids that I shared with my dad; one that was healthier, perhaps, but based on that same unconditional love and appreciation. And that was when I put it together. I knew I wanted to have children, but there was no way I was going to put them to bed at night with booze on my friggin' breath. I downed what must have been my tenth double vodka, straight up with a lemon, and stumbled out onto the beach.

In those days I believed in God, though my belief system was based mostly on guilt and the need to appease my father. I sprawled out on the sand and squinted to focus as I looked up into the heavens. There I saw an incredible bright light. It had a tail on it and was literally frozen in time. It was the Hale-Bopp Comet, though I was too drunk to put that together until I read about it in the paper the following day. Hawaii was one of the few places in the world where, for a certain amount of time, the comet appeared to be standing still in the sky in all its cosmic glory. Staring up at it, I began to weep. Not at its beauty, nor at a sudden acknowledgment of my alcohol issue, but at the fact that my waitress from the bar had just walked over to present my tab of $160.

It was April 12, 1997, and that was the last time I had a drink. Sure, there are those rare times when I miss it, like when I'm at a titty bar or when I'm forced to watch reality TV. But I never miss the dread, lost opportunities, embarrassed apologies, and self-punishment that every alcoholic has to endure. And it's nice to have a liver again. Those fuckers can really take a punch.

I wish I could give some advice to those struggling with addiction. I wish I could share some secret nugget about what got me straight, never to look back or never to fall off. But I just stopped. I knew I wouldn't have survived in the long haul if I didn't. Ironically and thankfully, my sobriety created an even greater freedom on- and offstage. I had convinced myself that the substances were giving me strength, but in reality, they were holding me back. They gave a false feeling of freedom, which only limited my potential for creativity, expression, and growth.

One tidbit I *can* offer to those in a similar predicament is to try and focus on gratitude in times of struggle. Whether you're grateful for your existence, your family, or being able to do what you love, there is power in acknowledging and appreciating what you have. Sure, there are times when I have a pity party for myself or get frustrated with my industry or my choices or whatever the case may be. But I try to let the low points last only a few minutes, and getting through them without a drink or a drug is the truest form of gratefulness. Sometimes I feel euphoric through simply doing the right thing. And I promise you, if you're good to yourself and stay thankful, it will pay off.

I only went to three A.A. meetings, and though I believe wholeheartedly in the twelve-step program, I was certain if I had to frequent those meetings that I would have ended up drinking even more. Hearing how a biker stabbed his girlfriend during a blackout gave me more anxiety when I had to walk alone to my car after a meeting. The key for me was quite simply not to drink. Everyone needs to get there in his or her own way. But if it's killing you or those around you, get there any way you can.

Clearly, entering middle age affords us plenty of opportunities to look back and reflect on the stuff we want to
carry into our second half, as well as the stuff we want to
leave behind. I've learned that people *can* change, but few
do because the hard work so often outweighs the desire. The
"old dog, new tricks" philosophy is accurate, though it can
double as a convenient copout. Like anything else in life, it
all comes down to how badly you want something.

Jill Diven (right) at the Rio Hotel, Las Vegas, 1997.

10

"A Sober Guy and a Cocktail Waitress Walk into a Bar . . ."

You have probably gathered by now that I have an addictive personality. That said, I don't consider myself a "recovering alcoholic." I consider myself a "former alcoholic." I know the folks at A.A. will disagree, and that's okay, because they obviously know a lot more about the condition than I do. But I'm not a former teenager; I'm an adult, right? I also don't believe that alcoholism is a disease. You can't stop a disease. You can stop being a drunk.

I often say that people with addictive and compulsive wiring will replace one addiction with another while combating their neurosis. I'm no doctor, but I do understand the beast, and I have years of experience with "stuffing the black hole," trying to artificially soothe and comfort my feelings of insecurity and self-doubt. Because this is not a self-help book, I'm allowed to make statements like that without giving evidence, answers, or solutions. I would rather refer to this as a *self-aware* book, actually.

The black hole is the place in your gut that cries out when you have feelings of inadequacy, guilt, anxiety, or sometimes just plain boredom (which, if you're like me, is often). In other words, we all have a black hole. It's bigger in some than in others, and how we choose to deal with it varies. Personally, I like to cram it with as much unimportant shit as possible, though with age (particularly middle age), it seems to be getting less and less cluttered. Other losers like to fill it up by working out and doing community service.

I'm a variety junkie. Variety in everything, especially food, women, projects, houses, and cars. There are books on the shelf selling right next to mine that will conclude these are the indications of an insecure, insatiable man. Others may say, "This fuck knows how to live," and I think both would be correct. But rest assured, these desires to change things up often are served with a side of enormous baggage.

Much of the planet, and most certainly towns like L.A., revolve around appearance and first-impression bullshit. Women are unfortunately expected to take this to a frightening level because we boys keep demanding bigger tits, tighter asses, and smaller dresses. That said, by God, we appreciate it! So thank you, ladies. Keep up the good work!

Admittedly, I feel grateful that my thirty-one-year-old girlfriend labors at the gym to keep her already great body in shape as I sit at home, writing this book and eating Fritos. But does that mean I join her at the gym? *Or* do I have a fish-and-chips dinner and look into buying a red sports car to fuel my inadequacy? Is it wrong to go after the more fun and satisfying outcome? "Vvvaaa-roooom" sounds much better than having Kronk at the gym yell, "Give me one more!" And that, my friends, is the beauty of growing older. "Who gives a fuck?" suddenly has a lovely ring to it, when just a few years ago it rang hollow, immature, and defensive. The difference now is that in some odd, indefinable way, I feel I've earned being able to say, "Fuck it."

As I mentioned, I've never been an A.A. guy, but I know one of the rules of the twelve-step program is to avoid getting into a serious relationship within the first two years of one's sobriety. That's a damn good one, though not always easy to follow. Especially when you're looking to "fill the hole," like I was. My synapses and chronically lonesome loins began to reappear, and my sobriety gave me a clarity and strength that made me feel more fearless than ever. I believed that I was ready to enter into a relationship because I was still a compulsive fuck, even though I had stopped boozing. I was far from having anything figured out.

When I was about six months sober, I began to experience a slight rebirth that is supposedly common around this period of dryness. I had a week hiatus from shooting *Raymond,* and I decided to take my pops to Vegas for a guys' weekend. We were playing low-stakes poker at the Rio when my future ex-wife, the lovely and statuesque Jill Diven, dipped and laid a double iced tea with extra lemons next to my paltry stack of chips. She handed my dad his fifth coffee. He tossed her a dollar chip with the flourish of Donald Trump. I glared at him as I slipped the temptress a green twenty-five-dollar chip. My dad glared back at me.

Jill was blond, blue-eyed, five-ten, and had the only real breasts on that shift. At least she did back then. She was shy, sweet, simple, and hard working. At least she was back then. And she smelled me coming a mile away in all of my bright-eyed wonderment and newfound clarity.

For some reason, I've dated a lot of waitresses over the years. Not sure why. Probably because of my insecurity, always needing to feel I had the upper hand, lessening the chance that I'd be dumped. That, and I think I took "liked to be waited on" to a new level. After a short two-month courtship and a lot of persuading on my part, Jill moved into my recently purchased home in the Hollywood Hills, just off of Sunset Boulevard. We couldn't have been more different on almost every level, and I'm sure she felt that way as well. But Jill being from humble beginnings in Pueblo, Colorado, and me needing to feel loved and important immediately, we plowed through with our eyes closed, never stopping to figure each other out. Though it was odd for me to dive into something so quickly, I believe my sobriety amped up my fear of being alone. And after getting to know Jill a little bit, I realized she hated being alone as well. "Any port in a storm," as my dad used to say.

Three months into our courtship, Jill found out she was pregnant, and we rushed into marriage in hopes of acquiring what I'd only dreamed of and never really had: a real family. I'm grateful every day because I was given my two amazing children, Max and Hope.

Unfortunately and predictably, our marriage started to crumble shortly into our fourth year, though we hung in there for seven. We found ourselves in something that felt like a long-distance thirty-year marriage. I was not a faithful husband, and the apathy on both sides was overwhelming. The bottom line was we were decent people who just didn't belong together.

I came to realize with insurmountable guilt and dread that I had repeated something from my own childhood that I had prayed never to encounter again: a divorce.

The day I sat down with my two young children to try and explain that Daddy was going to move out was the most painful day of my life. They were at those ages when it would never make sense to them, but they were old enough to experience the loss and pain.

Ironically, at the same time, my career was at its peak.

I had just won my third Emmy for *Raymond* and was appearing on Broadway alongside the great Nathan Lane and Matthew Broderick in *The Odd Couple*. But I was dying inside, because my lifelong unrealistic dream of being the perfect father was disintegrating before my eyes. In hindsight, I think maybe I wanted to be a parent more than a husband. What was important was figuring out what was best for everyone in the long term. As in all failed marriages, the tension between me and their mom would have been more devastating in time than the much needed separation, which has ultimately allowed us to become friends but, more importantly, better parents.

So here I was at forty-five, working to stay sober, experiencing partial erections, popping TUMS and antidepressants like mints, wondering where the fuck the years had gone, about to lose half of my dough-Ray-me to a cocktail waitress from Pueblo, Googling "chronic constipation," battling to maintain the love and respect of my children, and pretty much beginning to question EVERY LITTLE THING.

And now, as I hurl myself toward my mid-fifties, I find it imperative to share with all who will listen my twisted and skewed philosophy that appears to become more relevant as I grow older.

At my cousin's Bar Mitzvah, 1973.
Darren, seated, center. I'm the pimp on the right.

The Power of the Pink

Another good title for this chapter could be "The Art of Settling." Which reminds me of one of my favorite Elton John songs, "Rocket Man." There's a verse that says, "I miss the earth so much I miss my wife." I always took that literally, as in: "I miss the earth so much I *even* miss my wife." Elton purists may argue that it was meant to have a comma after the word "much," as if he'd been making a list of the things that he missed: earth, my wife, gravity, etc. The fact is, Elton was probably thrilled that he would never *have* to worry what it means, unless his partner happens to be the "wife" in their relationship, in which case my heart goes out to him.

Okay, relax, yes, there are good wives. I just think that

Sir Elton knew exactly what he was chirping about. "I *even* miss my wife. 'Cause it's just that fuckin' dark and lonely out here in space."

It pains me to reflect on how rich I'd be if I had said "I don't" instead of "I do."

I wouldn't be writing this book right now, that's for sure. If you happen to be sporting a penis, or at least the remnants of one after your female counterpart rearranged it into a nice little package, either from divorce or witchcraft, let me save you a bunch of time . . . and money. Women rule the world. As they should. End of story. The sooner you realize this, the sooner your man-sack can begin to heal.

Usually, "the power of the pink" is something that men find difficult to fully understand until they're middle-aged, *if* even then. My father was married six times, so he never really grasped it, but he proved time and again that women indeed run the show. That's why they carry the baby, hire the gardener, and pay the bills. They're better equipped on every level. Emotionally, spiritually, and strategically.

Learning about women is entirely on-the-job-training, and it takes about half a century to get it half right, assuming you're paying attention, which men usually are not. So if you're twenty-five, quit pretending you get women, because you don't get shit. I do. Somewhat. And I have the canceled checks to prove it.

Most men answer to a higher power, and it ain't heavenly, though the ladies will get you praying to the heavens quite frequently. Every man who has ever faltered, stumbled, or lost the rule of a country, his senate seat, his money, his identity, his career, his fucking mind, had a woman's prints all over him. Everything a man does: busting his ass at work, one hundred crunches in the morning, the Ferrari or the Kia he can't afford, the plugs in his head that make him look like he's growing corn, the man-girdle (yes, they have them), all that shit is done for the ladies. Why? Because that tiny area (bigger in European women) not only houses the future of the world but also has the strength to alter your mind. It doesn't help that men are pigs and typically not too instinctive, and that's why the women hold the keys to the trough.

I love it when guys say, "I wear the pants in the house," when in reality they only wear the pants that the Mrs. lays out for them on the bed. And when do they start laying out our clothes for us? Right around middle age, my friends. So wear the peach-colored slacks with the turquoise polo and shut the fuck up.

Men are ruled by their penis for the majority of their life, at least until their member starts to do them wrong. That transition usually occurs around midlife as well. And I believe this is all payback for how awfully we have treated our wiener over the years—worse than any other organ. We have neglected it, humiliated it, abused it, put it in peril, and don't get me started about the places we've shoved it or gotten it stuck. Thank goodness it only has one eye or it never would've been able to live with itself.

However, even when you're just under seven feet tall, like I am, if the schmekel is lacking, we must divert the eyes somewhere else, a penile sleight-of-hand, if you will. This could also be the reason I always seemed to date smaller women. Simply for the selfish reason of my penis appearing larger. But that usually backfired. As they say in the medical field, "Big woman, big vagina. Small woman, all vagina."

I so welcomed the day when I finally came out of the ether and discovered there were other things just as important (or perhaps even more enticing) than rolling over and asking someone, "Did you finish?" Like, for example, the butter cake at Mastro's, or taking a good dump after Super Bowl Sunday, or maybe finding the one pair of shoes that don't hurt my hammertoe. These have become the happy places since my dick took the turn.

The nice thing about hitting middle age is it becomes significantly clear that the uneven playing field you and your partner have rallied on for decades is starting to level out, if only by a little. That's why the second marriage is often the keeper. Not because it's that much better, but because you have grown up a bit to understand that a good marriage is nothing more than both parties giving up simultaneously. You must quit as a team in order to make the grade. Looking at each other and then yourselves in the mirror with death-defying honesty and admitting, "Where the fuck am I going?" is the only path to true bliss. So you might as well hunker down, learn to say yes, and pray for sudden hearing loss, which statistically and ironically starts around your fifties.

But as you settle into the inevitable, continue to remember that the ladies own it, run it, and invented it. I think it's called a monopoly. And there's nothing wrong with that. Just be aware of it and not surprised when it hits you hard in the wallet on anniversaries or in divorce court. Because men will pay for it one way or another time and time again, so it must be worth it, right? You have one gigolo for every hundred thousand hookers, and we all know figures don't lie.

How many women do you know who pay spousal support? (Ellen or Rosie O'Donnell don't count, even though they're technically women.) Alimony? You mean I even have to pay for the person I don't want anymore because I was generous while trying to keep her happy during better times? And now I'm being penalized for that?

What I noticed after my divorce, while I was forced to keep my ex in the same "lifestyle she was accustomed to," was that *my* lifestyle had to come down a notch or two while she continued to live high on the hog without ever contributing financially. My career was far along and successful way before we met, so how does it compute that she (or any ex-wife or ex-husband) gets to reap the benefits without having anything to do with the source? It's kind of like paying for the lease on a car after turning it in, while someone else is driving it. The game has changed regardless of whose fault it is, though it's ultimately both or mostly mine, depending on who you ask. The breadwinner is the sole reason the spouse became "accustomed" to anything in the first place. And for the women who financially take care of their men, the same should apply for them, whoever they are.

Please understand I'm only referring to crazy alimony. Any father who bails on child support is a scumbag. Period. I judge a man on the father he is before anything else. If you can't love and support your kids, keep your dick in the drawer. If you want to help out the Betty after the divorce, good for you, but it's also okay for her to go out there and get a job. Like she did. Before you met. Please understand, I'm not bitter. I'm better . . . equipped. Or I will be if I come back as a woman.

You want to know what's fair? Everyone leaves with *what they came with*. Period. You both have to start over, so *start over*! Fellas, I beg you, get a prenup. If she doesn't understand why you want it, then you have the wrong broad. It's about protection and reality, because at the end of the day, *people change*. And they really change when they're pissed, or lied to, or confronted, or bored, or scorned.

I once heard a woman say, "If he wants a prenup, it just shows he doesn't believe in us or doesn't trust me." To that, I say, if you don't feel you should sign it, then it's all about the money from the start. Don't you love your partner enough that you want him or her to feel protected? Where's the love? For richer or poorer, if you believe in the two of you like you say, then it's just a gesture of goodwill, right?

It's not a gold rush, ladies. I speak the truth with firsthand knowledge.

A woman will cost you more than any drug addiction, gambling binge, real estate debacle, or frivolous lawsuit. You will lose your mind if she wants you to, along with all your lettuce. That's why the vagina is shaped like that, so you can swipe your credit card. One-stop shopping for eternity. If she's Jewish, swipe once and wait for approval. Asian, swipe it sideways, backside up. Mexican, you'll need two forms of ID. If she's from the South, make sure it doesn't eat your card. If it does, do *not* put your dick in there! That's right, I said it.

Shannon Treglia

My chickens — Hope (left, one year old) and Max (right, two and a half), 2001.

12

"Because I Said So."

I think it's safe to say that parenting skills are not genetically inherited. Especially in my case. By all means, my parents did the best they could, but some stuff I'm certain was not passed down. I think it's also safe to say that each generation inherently repeats parts of its own childhood in some ways, and overcompensates for shortcomings in others. My mom would unplug her phone when she went to bed, even with three teenage boys going in and out of the house. I have tracking devices on my kids' phones so I know where they are at every waking moment. Surely there's a happy medium.

Here's a slice of my childhood to give you a point of comparison. My best friend growing up was Jeremy Wallen. He loved fucking with me because I was the perfect kid to play practical jokes on: I already came equipped with a good amount of anxiety. We used to walk home from school together, but one day in October, he didn't wait for me and purposely beat me home. His dad had just gotten him a gorilla suit for Halloween, and Jeremy had a perfect plan. He ran over to my house dressed in the suit, with the gorilla head under his arm, and rang my doorbell. He caught my mom between naps and asked her if I was home. Mom said, "I don't think so, darling, not yet. I don't smell Pop-Tarts."

Jeremy said, "Great! Mind if I hide in his bedroom closet?"

Mom said, "Sure."

Try and grasp the dysfunction. After thirty years of therapy, my shrink still comes up dry. Moments later, I walked my lanky ass into my room, threw my books on the bed, examined a zit in my mirror, and BANG, Jeremy bolted from my closet in full gorilla regalia. As my girlish screams turned into wailing, I shoved my mom toward the gorilla and fled the house at a speed never to be equaled by any white man . . . as I was peeing. That's right. I said it. Fuck you, too. I was eleven! I ran halfway down the block until I collapsed with exhaustion. Jeremy wasn't far behind, with his elfish laugh coming from under the rubber mask. I could have killed the little prick, but he definitely would have kicked my ass.

In case you're not quite clear on what a Jewish mother is like, this will help you grasp the mind-set attributed to the breed. What was my mother's comment when I returned home, seething with anger and smelling of piss? She said, "I can't believe you would push your own mother into a gorilla." I didn't close my closet doors for three months.

Upon becoming a father for the first time, I quickly learned there is nothing as powerful as the love for your child. But it is without a doubt the toughest gig in the world if you're doing it right. I think this level of dedication comes from a certain kind of chip that is found more often in females than in males. It's a caregiving attribute that I truly feel is in the DNA. I will never forget the day my son was born and I cut the cord, uttering the words, "It's a pound over, shall I wrap it?" Or that day in December 2001, when my daughter took her first step, teetered, fell forward, and then puked on my new Italian slip-ons.

I learned early on that there is nothing as unbridling and forthright as a child's honesty. Especially compared to a parent's. Ironically, kids are also the most brilliant liars next to politicians. My son at age five actually once told me, after hitting his sister, that "God told him to." An unsettling lie that made me rethink the theory of evolution. What if the kid was right? He is known to move in mysterious ways. This was the same kid who told the waitress at IHOP that "Daddy farted in the car on the way to breakfast." An unfortunate truth that has destroyed my love of pancakes and Sunday drives.

I once caught my four-year-old daughter chasing her big brother with a bat because he put a booger on her Malibu Barbie. Thank goodness I caught her in midswing as I cried bloody hell. When I questioned her intention with saliva propelling from my mouth, her excuse was "I was just seeing how heavy the bat was, Daddy. I'd never hit him." Uh-huh. As much as we love them, they are most definitely out to kill us.

You will be astonished at how many things your kids can break, lose, throw, and just plain fuck up in a matter of minutes. Remotes in the toilet; tuna in your shoe; ice cream on the dog; a flashlight in the aquarium. All things that make you ponder a vasectomy with the intensity of a jet fighter. An argument between your kids in the backseat of the van after a ten-hour day at Disneyland will make you decide: "I am letting someone take a knife to my testicles and tie the arteries to my balls so I will never have to relive this day." And I thought it was the happiest place on earth. To quote one of my heroes, Rodney Dangerfield, "Now I know why tigers eat their young."

I almost gave myself the procedure inadvertently one day when I was putting the Christmas ornaments away in the attic. I was in the farthest part of the attic that I could find, because let's face it, being a Jew, I wasn't supposed to be playing with that shit in the first place, right? Being totally unaware how an attic is constructed, I decided I would straddle a large beam to secure my stability. As foot left and foot right stepped onto the ceiling drywall to balance my jumbo frame, well, I guess there's no other way to say it: my balls broke my fall. I landed squarely with my friggin' plums on the beam, and as my legs, covered in red sweatpants, shot through the ceiling above where my four-year-old son was playing with his new train set, I vaguely heard him yell, "Santa's back!" "Vaguely," I say, because I almost passed out from the impact. If I had been lucky enough to miss the beam, I would have fallen through a different part of the ceiling and encountered a thirty-foot drop. Had that happened, I would be writing this by holding a pencil in my mouth. Tough to erase stuff that way.

The key to parenthood is not only having a great nanny who can't write English (thus sparing you the possibility of a tell-all book) but also the ability to be a great friend to your kids without being their best friend. You're a parent first, a friend second, a slave third, a defendant fourth. They are sponges who will illuminate your faults and elevate your talents. They will get the runs at the worst possible times and make you drive them around at three A.M. as if you've forgotten where you live, just so they'll fall asleep. Your life, as you know it, will be over. And you will spend the next twenty years trying to regain what you once had. You will experience a lot less fun but a lot more joy.

Before my seed ever found purchase, whenever I heard about a guy becoming a father at fifty or sixty years of age, I would think, *What a selfish bastard. His kid will be ten and he'll be seventy!* After becoming a father, I now think, *That guy is a genius.* He figured out that by the time his kids are teenagers, he'll be battling dementia, in a coma, or dead. Sitting shell-shocked in a home, eating pudding with no teeth, unaware that his teenage son put something on Instagram that is unrecognizable unless you turn it upside down and close one eye. "Out of sight if you're out of your mind," I always say. Have them late in life and your excuses for bad parenting are endless *and* validated.

I'm always amazed at the clueless parents who expect random people in public to put up with their kid's shit. The ones who leave brutal messes under their child's highchair for the poor restaurant server to deal with after Chucky throws all his uneaten crap on the floor. The relentless screamer with the parents who act like they can't fuckin' hear it. Take them outside for a walk until they chill out, Trailer Trash. Pretend you give a shit. The crier on the plane? Shouldn't be allowed, sorry. I have kids. Bring shit for them to do and to eat. Yes, their ears will sometimes hurt, and I know that's a bitch, but pull your tit out and make the plane happy. You squirted him out, we didn't. My earbuds are only so big. And who knows, maybe the consideration for others will eventually rub off on your offspring.

As the saying goes, there's nothing more fun than seeing the world through the eyes of a child. Yet I believe this phrase was written by a child. It's not always that fun. It's at least much better than through the eyes of a guy hitting "the double nickel," which is where I find myself today. But every stage has its challenges, even though I did my best to prevent my children from all forms of adversity. I was determined to be with my children through every possible step in their young lives. I tried to predict accidents before they would happen. I wrapped my house in Styrofoam, padding, and duct tape so every slip and fall would be bolstered with a cushy landing. My tendency was to be what many experts refer to as a "helicopter parent," always checking, fixing, and planning. I wanted their lives to have the structure that my early years lacked. And sometimes, through that desire, I oversteered or unconsciously robbed them of the experience that comes from things not being perfect or easy. I overcompensated because of my feelings of guilt fueled from my divorce. At times I acted like a damn teenager myself.

Being a father was so important to me that I had times when I forgot to *breathe*. Forgot it the other night, when my kids decided to fry Oreos in hot vegetable oil in a skillet. Not sure why. They didn't see it on the Food Network; they weren't even high. Just had a great idea that resulted in a grease fire that was quickly doused with water. Which my teenage kids, both in chemistry, didn't know could lead to an even worse fire. I took a breath and ended up spurting out more F-bombs than Kanye's box set. Yes, my heart has been mostly in the right place since that day in October 1998 when I became a dad. And again in February 2000. Learn from me, if you're a parent or planning to become one when you hit sixty-five, do your best, and also know you can only do so much. There will be times when you will save the day, and also times when you'll be the biggest dick in the room. In a bad way. But if you can teach your kids two things, aim for *compassion* and *courage,* two crucial ingredients that are missing all too often in this world.

One way in which parents attempt to teach compassion is by buying a pet. We think it will teach them responsibility, but we all know how that turns out. The first pet I ever bought for my kids was a hermit crab. It's either that or the carnival goldfish, which has the life expectancy of a hiccup. After unsuccessfully dropping fifty dollars at the Ping-Pong-ball-goldfish-toss, we headed to Petco.

These days it appears to be okay to decorate hermit crab shells using various types of (what I'm hoping is) nontoxic paint. Ours had a tiny lighthouse and beach painted on its shell, I guess to make him even more homesick for his better days. We purchased the hermit habitat along with the food, the tiny sponge that needed to remain wet, "special" sand, and a ceramic sailboat: again to remind him of his life a few weeks ago at Martha's Vineyard. The whole setup cost around eighty dollars. If we could have just won that fish . . .

The kids named him or her Shelly, and they used to fight over whose room it would sleep in. Until they stopped arguing and agreed to share, Shelly would sleep in my room. That arrangement lasted only a couple of days. What I didn't know was that these fuckers are nocturnal and scrape and scratch around at night. Me being a light sleeper, Shelly soon became a kitchen dweller.

What the guy at the pet store never bothered to mention was that hermit crabs grow out of their shells. Apparently, a bigger shell needed to be purchased and put in the tank for Shelly's inevitable move on up to the east side. Honestly, if the clerk *had* shared this info on the day of purchase, I probably would have looked at him strangely, like the cynical guy I am, because let's be honest, who the hell would think that a hermit crab would need a newer, bigger shell? Dogs don't grow out of their coats, right?

Sure enough, after about four months, we find one morning over breakfast that Shelly has vacated her shell. Have you ever seen a hermit crab sans shell? You may never eat popcorn shrimp again. Horrifying. At this point I had no idea about the crab needing new digs. We assumed she was stepping out to get some fresh air, and figured she'd go back in her shell at night, like all good crustaceans. Unfortunately, this didn't happen. Once a hermit crab leaves a shell, it never returns. Kind of like the ghetto. Mind you, this was before Google, so we thought all was okay until the next day, when we noticed that Shelly had lost a leg. The day after that, another leg was gone, and so on. It was like Hanukkah, *Sopranos*-style.

Shelly was failing, and the cage began to smell like Red Lobster. When the kids were in school, like most good parents, I rushed to the pet store to inquire why the crab was shedding appendages. I was hoping they would grow back, like a lizard's tail. No such luck for Shelly. They explained to me what they failed to explain the first time around. A new Shelly was purchased, along with a larger spare shell. Painted on her shell were palm trees and a coastal sunset.

Recently, I found myself in a public restroom at a restaurant with another dad who had a teenage son. After the teenager peed, he went to leave and the father said, "Aren't you going to wash your hands?"

With that typical teenage attitude, the son said, "The sign says you only have to do it if you work here."

My son, Max, is sixteen and my daughter, Hope, is fifteen, and I have to say, I have loved every stage of their childhoods. I changed their diapers and took the feeding shifts at night and reveled in the process. My nipples still hurt. Those early days are when the real bonding happens, so it's important for fathers to take part in caring for their kids early on.

All things considered, I'm surviving the teenage years quite well. Their mother and I do all we can to keep them busy and keep them talking. Trust is the key in any parent-child dynamic, but trust must be earned, and it's hard to balance that with the certain amount of privacy they need and deserve. Sure, we've had our difficulties, like all families, but my best times are when they're by my side. My excitement for their future revolves around their discoveries and growth as young, positive-thinking individuals empowered by their self-esteem and the willingness to pursue careers fueled by love and passion for whatever they choose. These are my desires and wishes for my children.

In closing this chapter I want to mention that I started my own nonprofit organization called Maximum Hope Foundation back in 2000. We provide immediate, practical assistance to families who are caring for a child with a life-limiting illness, and we're doing some pretty amazing work nationwide. To learn more, please take a moment to visit our website (www.MaximumHopeFoundation.org).

13

Adam and Eve Had No Chance

Whether or not you believe in the Bible, the story of Adam and Eve proves that even God Himself doubted the long-lasting union of He and She. Sure, He made a big deal about marriage, but if He thought people were *naturally* designed to stay together, He wouldn't have needed to make such a big deal of the whole "bound for eternity" thing. It also appears that "the man upstairs" is living single there among the clouds, which drives home my point. I could be wrong, but I've never heard of a Godette or Mrs. God, and if the most powerful being in the universe decides to remain unattached, there must be something to that. He's obviously not buying the "Till death do you part" crap. Therefore, neither do I.

Poor Adam and Eve were doomed from the start. "Don't eat from this tree; watch out for that snake; don't touch my fig leaf." Fucking rules that were impossible to follow out of the gate. And they paid for it dearly "in the beginning," just like the Good Book says.

It's amazing that we live in a country where same-sex marriage is such an issue when opposite-sex marriages fail 85 percent of the time. We have more in common with our own genders than we do with our opposite, meaning the chips are stacked against us early on. We've covered the "power of the pink" and the innate differences between men and our great rulers, the broads. When I became a father, my hypothesis about the sexes became more concrete than ever. Our inherent gender conflicts are deeply rooted in our DNA.

Most little girls by age three or four are fascinated with caregiving and nurturing. Their first toy is usually a dolly or stuffed animal that they bring to tea parties with their other toys or playmates. They get a stroller or a highchair for their baby; the baby is coddled, bathed, and fed; and their tenderness is purely instinctual. Boys, on the other hand, spend the first seven to eight years of their lives (twenty if they're Catholic) holding on to their penises. Sometimes it's for fun, or out of habit, or perhaps a natural reaction to feeling anxiety at the zoo. Or the airport. Or Hickory

Farms. They have a death grip on their little buddy and are never really sure why.

Here's a transcript of a conversation at the mall between my seven-year-old son, his mom, and me:

Me: Why are you holding your penis?

Son: You mean right now?

Me: Yes. And on and off for the last few years.

Ex-wife: What's the big deal, Brad? Relax.

Me: I'm very relaxed. Not relaxed enough to hold my member for the better part of the day, but relaxed nonetheless. Do you have to pee, son?

Son: No. I'm good.

Me: Okay, great. Then give it a rest. Let it breathe . . .

Son: But it itches.

Me: Maybe that's because it's allergic to your hand?

Ex-wife: Are you serious? What are you, jealous?

Me: Of what?!

Ex-wife: Just leave it alone.

Me: Tell *him* to leave it alone.

Son: It's *my* wiener!

And therein lies the rub, no pun intended. It is indeed his wiener. The only organ that will burn through his finances, promote insane decisions, and wreak continuous havoc. And as a young boy, he already knows this. That's why we guys hold on to it for dear life. Because in a few years, it will be set free and unmanageable, never to return again, gone forever as it rules over its cousin, the larger head, from its ironically smaller, lower throne.

The fact is, we're born pre-wired. Pre-wired for success, death, rashes, multiple marriages, heart conditions, ass-cancer, schizophrenia, lactose intolerance, bunions, penal curvature, addiction, baldness, incontinence, and excessive earwax. It's also the reason a colonel in the army can have a son who's a florist. Yes, I believe that trait is predetermined genetics as well.

I am not an expert on anything, and I'm sure by now that has become very clear. Yet I do believe that I'm a very old soul. Over my past lives, I have had countless failed relationships on four different continents, in six separate eras, including Ancient Rome, Pre-Plastics, Disco, and one specific occasion wherein I overheard Henry Ford make some anti-Semitic remarks to my mistress while fixing her steam engine.

I am a member of the Mile High Club if you count masturbation. I've only had crabs once and I deserved it. I lost my virginity two weeks shy of my fifteenth birthday to a gorgeous twenty-eight-year-old woman who was simultaneously having a high-profile affair with a married D.C. politician. This became big news on the Hill and landed her in *Playboy*. I was introduced to the gal by my dad, which was odd, but in his defense, he was dating her girlfriend, and I looked nineteen, and one thing led to another. Okay, yeah, it's still odd. But it's greatly appreciated.

I've been in love six times, lived with four women, and been cash-poor more than a dozen times. My cohabitating experience is vast and my mistakes have been stellar, but I can't stress enough that the only way you can survive marriage is by being fuckin' honest with yourself before saying "I do." Are you getting married because it's what you want? Or do you feel pressured by external forces to take that leap? Are you prepared to risk your physical freedom, your fortune, your sexual frequency, your privacy, your power, and your ability to choose your own clothes, food, and weekend activities? Once you've determined your true level of commitment, if you still decide to move forward with the union, then you must realize the importance of being "only as honest as you need to be" with your partner. Ignorance is bliss indeed, and it may end up being the only bliss that your relationship contains. Don't feel the need to tell your soul mate everything. You need to tell your *cell mate* everything. Big difference.

Women invented weddings, of that I am sure. That's why you've never seen a magazine called *Groom*. The flowers, the dress, the invites, the music, the food, the seating arrangements—how many of the guy's ideas are incorporated? Where are the foosball, buffalo wings, and topless caterers? I rest my case. And most guys will say they don't care about that stuff. If you don't care, why do it at all? Because you love her so much you want her to be happy, right? Happy for how long, is the question. Meanwhile, you look like you're dressed for a funeral. Interesting, isn't it?

The bachelor party was designed for one reason: to remind you of what you're leaving behind. FUN. Fun with friends, booze, and broads without a curfew—the very fiber of what makes us men! Is she worth it? Maybe. *Forever* worth it? I think you know that answer. In other words, she's the "one and only" *today*. And that's great. But do me one favor when you're walking down the aisle and everyone in attendance knows you don't have a shot in hell of lasting into the next decade: bring half of the shit you own down the aisle with you. Just to be proactive. She's gonna get it anyway, so you might as well save money on movers. Bring a U-Haul, not a limo.

Something helpful that middle age has taught me is to agree with my significant other more than ever. Not because I've lost my balls but because I don't have the energy to debate the obvious, and knowing I'm right without having to verbalize it is enough. This concept is rather advanced and more of a female tactic, but since they're usually smarter, let us learn from that and steal the idea. As we age, I feel honesty loses its value anyway. My rec-

ommendation is to save it for the witness stand. And by
your fifties, your memory is a crapshoot at best, so what is
honesty then? It's simply what you remember. Or better
yet, *choose* to remember. "I don't remember that" said by
a middle-ager is not only valid but probable. Say it in your
thirties and you're dead.

Think back on the biggest fights you ever had with your
spouse. Most likely they started from someone being bru-
tally honest. What the hell for? To gain brownie points? To
feel superior? To relieve guilt for that sedative you slipped
your mother-in-law? Fuck that. Most folks are allergic to the
truth. Find that shit out before walking down the aisle, because you've got a sure death sentence if you don't. Your
only other option is to memorize the following comments,
which can be used on an as-needed basis (they're unisex unless otherwise noted):

"No, you don't look fat in that dress/jacket."

"You'd never know your brother/sister is schizophrenic.
He/she is a delight!"

"I try not to eat red meat."

"I've never done this before."

"Size doesn't matter."

"I have to stay late at work even though I miss you madly."

"You're ten times cuter than your best friend."

"Why in the hell would I cheat on you with someone not
nearly as pretty/handsome? Come on!"

"Karen has big tits? I didn't notice." (For men/lesbians only.)

"You're much better endowed than that NFL player I dated." (For women/gay men only.)

"Let's sleep in the guestroom and give your uncle with anal leakage our bed."

"You're just better at doing it."

"I'm proud of you for trying."

"We need to get away. Soon."

"*Oprah*'s the shit./*The Godfather* is the shit."

"I feel you're safer in *your* car."

"You're right." (Optional add-on: "As usual.")

This is how you keep it together later in life. Can you do it? Do you want to? Because bottom line is, you're gonna need to. It's our early-in-life ego that makes us think we'll get through it on our terms. Or that we'll change them. There are no terms, and there is no changing, there are only rock-hard rules. If you don't know this by midlife, I suggest you get ready to write a big, fat check.

Luckily, later in life, libido starts to diminish. But rarely does this happen at the same time as your partner's. When the sex goes away or takes on different forms known as the "appreciative hand job," the "dutiful quickie," or the "incoherent blow job," all bets are off. At that point you need to turn your attention to the garage, the pantry, or ESPN. Can you do that? Are you ready? Can you act excited about her scrapbooking? Your level of enthusiasm may be directly proportional to how much genital atten-tion you'll receive, so you'd better learn to bump it up, my friend. Will you be able to throw on that neon-yellow sweater because that same mother-in-law you roofied is coming over for Easter brunch? She bought it for you, bitch, so you better man up and put it on just to make your life flow easier. And as we learn in our later years, it's all about the flow, Joe.

I've made a few enemies when it comes to expressing my thoughts on marriage. I do believe in true love; I do believe that some folks are meant to be together; I do not believe in "till death do us part." This is not pessimism so much as it is an acknowledgment that we continue to evolve, grow, decay, change, and fall in and out of love. If you both do these things in the same direction, simultaneously, good for you. But it's highly unlikely. I'm sorry, but I need more than a promise to get through the long haul. Divorce is at an all-time high for a reason: marriage is hard as shit. True, some people are more monogamous than others. I wish I were one of them. The fundamental issue is that women want security and men want excitement. Sure, women may want excitement and men may want security, but usually, they fall lower on the respective scales of importance. I'm a die-hard romantic. I'm also a relentless flirt. It's not that I don't believe in commitment; it's just that I think we place too much value on ceremonial bullshit and not enough on the reality of human nature.

The bottom line is, if you want to give any long-term relationship a shot, memorize those quotes above and practice them often to see how they land. It won't be easy at first, and if you say any of them with a grin, you're screwed.

So much for Adam and Eve. It's obvious that if they really existed, we would all be inbred disasters looking very much alike and adept at playing the fiddle. I've only found three states in the nation where these characteristics are prevalent. I need more evidence than that.

14

Celebrating Your E.D.
During Your Midlife Crisis

It shouldn't surprise you by this point that I believe the midlife crisis is an extension (or nonextension) that originates from the loins—or, more technically, our old friend the penis. In our early years he works too fast, in our prime years he wants to work too much, in our later years he refuses to work even when we beg, and in our final years he's just praying for good health insurance. Erectile dysfunction, or E.D., as it's known to the underworld, is broken into three major categories: Premature Ejaculation; Non-Erectus Minimus; and Curvature Morphesus, which is the least common of the three but also the most valuable. With Curvature Morphesus, you have to enter your partner from a forty-five-degree angle at a high rate of speed. But let's cover the first two, since they are more prevalent in the Caucasian world.

Premature Ejaculation and Non-Erectus Minimus are commonly referred to by women as "I wasn't even close to being done" and "Oh, so now you're not attracted to me anymore?" The life span between the decline of one and the onset of the other can be mere moments. If you are currently in that legendary, blissful in-between space, please, for the love of God, go out and take advantage of it as much as you possibly can.

Due to the fact that these conditions are quite natural over the course of one's lifetime, it's unfortunate that they get such a bad rap. Perhaps because the topics are a little too close to home? Granted. I recall that once during a specific interlude in my youth, I reached orgasm so quickly that I actually time-traveled. I opened my eyes, and suddenly I was a young knight getting my steed a drink from a moat, and my lady was running off with a stable hand. By the same token, I now have to pop two Cialis just to find my dick in the shower.

As most physicians will agree, premature ejaculation is not only common among millions of high school students but looked upon as good luck to Japanese businessmen visiting Norway. But is there a greater compliment you can give your partner than proving to her that you are so incredibly turned on, she need not even show up? What am I missing? Do we need to put a timetable on ecstasy? Has the world really come to that? The only reason women don't have the joy of premature orgasm is that they don't let themselves go there. Everything has to be finely orchestrated like a three-act opera.

Take a close look at the animal kingdom. Horse, spider, woodchuck—under two minutes and it's "let's hit the barn for some grub." Why? Because they are egoless creatures with no hang-ups. To them, the gift is just showing up. The *real* orgasm? Grub back at the barn. I hear there is nothing more wonderful than elongated intercourse, but whatever happened to "The early bird catches the worm" and "tick tock, motherfucker"? Come on, ladies, start without me and I'll "come in for the close" like the good car salesman I am.

I believe the phrase "midlife crisis" was coined not by a psychiatrist but by a jealous married guy. The yellow sports car, the young girlfriend, the new skull necklace . . . where's the crisis? This is all the shit the married guy probably doesn't have but deep down really wants. Of course, he'll deny this because his wife may be listening, but every man goes through the feelings of a midlife crisis if not necessarily the actions. It's in our DNA and conducive to our evolution. And why not? We figure we've lived on this planet for half a century, taken a lot of shit, worked our asses off, and maybe lost everything to the first wife or even the second one.

"I've earned my crisis and I'm damn well having one," you may lament. In other words, *"I want mine."* You know you'll never be that young stud again, but maybe you can temporarily latch on to that young damsel who can briefly remind you of your better days, if only for ten thousand dollars a month. What's the crisis? It's a diversion from reality, but so is your toupee that makes you look like a moron. Or those snow-white fake teeth. Or her rubber lips and fake tits. Why are those considered okay and not crises? When women do this stuff, it's called a second chance at life, a renaissance or a reckoning, or Eat, Love, and Pray, or some bullshit like that. Well, we want our time, too. That's why we love Jack Nicholson, Mick Jagger, Jeff Bridges, and the pope. They have it all, and they stare youth right in the peepers and say, "Fuck you."

Personally, I've inhabited both beings. I was the envious married guy and the midlife seeker of all that was shiny and curvy. Quite honestly, neither worked for me in the long term, but the short term was a *blast*. Zero regrets. Unfortunately, they both left me feeling empty because they lacked the authenticity of who I really was. And since I'm a comedian, both scenarios made it easier to make fun of myself.

I discovered Viagra in my early forties in hopes of giving my future plaintiff more pleasure. Or maybe it was the unabashed embarrassment of not being able to get a hard-on, I can't remember. Now in my mid-fifties, I need the little blue patch instead of the little blue pill; something that's pumped into my bloodstream so heavily that an issue of *AARP The Magazine* can get me off. Viagra has become a prerequisite to jacking off. I have to fool my dick into thinking it's not really me. I'm not sure if it's shame or disgust, but my hand seems to want to see other people and just be friends. Maybe just cuddle. I have actually seen my hand telling my dick, "It's not you, it's me."

My physician warned me that it's easy to take too many Viagra and that larger quantities could result in a painful four-to-five-hour erection. "Painful for whom?" I inquired.

"If that happens, you need to go to the emergency room or urgent care, seriously."

"Why?" I asked.

"Because it hurts like crazy and you could end up with gangrene," he replied. That was enough for me. That was when I decided to take only three at a time. After all, what's more embarrassing than walking into the ER with a blazing hard-on, crying out for help? Can't imagine they'd see me before the guy with the head wound. Unless I opened with "Please, I need help! Can somebody blow me? I need a nurse, and this time not Steve!"

I heard from a friend who works in an ER that they have to give the penis a shot of some kind when it won't retract. Not sure what they shoot it with. Probably a dose of marriage.

Luckily for women, as they age, at least their vaginas stay relatively consistent as far as working order and shape. Yes, they may start to resemble the Dust Bowl of the late 1800s, but it's still possible to navigate, with a little ingenuity, imagination, and a vat of chicken schmaltz. Guys, on the other hand, often lose that stiff wind that blew us into town, never to return without the help of Big Pharma. You wake up one morning and you're fifty and your little buddy is a stranger. Like an old, uninterested mistress. Or an antiquated Christmas ornament that you forgot to take down from the backdoor, lifelessly dangling in the breeze—weathered, partially discolored, and pissed. "I've been used," it says as it stares back at you in the mirror. "You only wanted me for sex." Deep down, you know it's right. Age has cheated you both. Your dick even has its own tiny beer belly. We call that the "dick gut." It's that second bulge under your stomach, just above the penis, where your pelvic bone used to hang out. Not anymore. Now it's like a fleshy fanny pack but without pockets and with even less dignity. You're like two twins, separated at birth by two guts. One gets hurt, the other one cries. My point is that evolution is kinder to the ladies. Got saggy boobs? Get a tit job. Got a saggy penis? Too bad.

15

Dating after Forty-Five

Dating when you're middle-aged means you bring to the table a plethora of experience that it would have been impossible to possess earlier in life. And with that experience comes the luxury of lowering the bar, along with your expectations. At this point in your life, you should have nothing to prove and no one to impress. The opposite sex must lower their bar as well so the food chain can shift dramatically. It's either that or everyone ends up alone.

Blind dates become much more prevalent in this stage of life (for good reason), and online dating has several advantages as well. The best part about dating at this age is that you have so many more excuses to bail when the fit isn't right. When you're twenty-six and you cancel because you're "not feeling well," she knows for a fact you're full of shit. If you cancel at fifty-three, the excuses are endless and most likely probable. You will have at least three medical conditions to point to, as well as memory loss, sudden death of a friend, irritable bowel syndrome (my favorite go-to; usually buys me a week), your own sudden death, forgetting where you parked, and numbness of the lower extremities.

If you find yourself dating at this point in your life, you have two choices: stay within your generation or go for someone you have no right being with but feel you've finally earned. I recommend the latter because you've most likely tried the other and it led to a divorce, boredom, hatred, or all of the above, so what have you got to lose? Pray you find someone who does not rely on your body or personality as the attraction, because one is shot and the other is warped. Maybe she'll like you for your money, or your boat, or the cabin in Aspen. It's all good. That's why you got that shit in the first place, remember? To attract the pink, get into a relationship where you can say, "We're using each other and we're fine with it." It doesn't get healthier than that.

You never hear a fifty-year-old say, "I hope to settle down with my best friend." That's thirtysomething bullshit. At fifty, you most likely already have a best friend or two. Now it's time for someone who isn't expecting much, has her own independence, and will let you take the A-Train once every couple months, regardless of her age.

Ironically, the truest love of my life, IsaBeall, is twenty-four years my junior. And no, that's not why she's the love of my life. But it helps. I fell right into the stereotype that I used to make fun of in my act, and now I have a slew of jokes shining a light on our age difference. How she colors the menu when we go out to dinner; the way her big-girl shoes light up when she walks; how a game of "got your nose" is considered foreplay; how we met when I got her Frisbee out of the tree; how she accidentally triggered an Amber Alert when we went to a movie.

Just because you're older doesn't mean you can't aim for the man or woman of your dreams, but be realistic about it. If Izzy dumps me for a thirty-year-old stud, you'll never be able to say, "I bet Brad didn't see that coming." Of course I saw it coming, you idiots! Maybe I didn't welcome it with open arms, but I sure got it, because I was once thirty. Not a stud, but thirty nonetheless. Love is ageless. Just like sliding down a hill in a cardboard box or jumping up and down on your orthopedic bed. If your back is fine with it, it may be worth trying. But it doesn't make sense to put a number on love. As far as I'm concerned, all are welcome.

I entered into this relationship as an opportunity to enjoy a young, beautiful woman for what it was worth. But I ended up being broadsided by the greatest heart and soul I have ever encountered. None of it would have been possible if I hadn't risked, expected nothing, and thought out of the box like a lecherous old man. Ironically, she is the *first* woman I've ever had a serious relationship with who adores her father and vice versa. So much for younger women dating older guys because of their daddy issues.

We all know that sex sells. That could be why I've had to start over financially several times. There are two kinds of sexual people: those who want it and those who use it to get what they want. And you can't have one without the other, right? But as a society, we must begin to give it a lot less weight. We must make it a common courtesy. A gesture of goodwill. We must get to the point where it's brief and recreational. The less attached we are, the clearer we can think. Is she really that good for me? Why did she laugh during foreplay? And where exactly was that humming coming from?

Let's go back to the animal kingdom for some more tips. Every wild and domesticated animal on earth is able to engage in sex without the mind-fuck that accompanies the act in the human world. Many scientists say that is because the only reason species engage in sex is to mate, and the act has nothing to do with egocentric pleasure. Really? Then maybe you can explain to me why my dog insists on humping the ottoman or licking his balls until he falls asleep. Is he that fucking stupid to think his gyrations will lead to procreation? Or maybe the scientists can explain why a cat walks back and forth against a drape until she looks like she needs a cigarette.

The Brothers Glib, (from left to right) Paul, me, and Jeff.

Left to right: Al (Dad), Dina (his 6th wife), Bert Convy's love child, Lionel (stepdad), and Barbara (Mom) in Reno, Nevada, 1987.

First nightclub gig, 1976.

Left to right: Rick Ducommun, Mark Pittu, Ed McMahon, Glenn Hirsh, and me on *Star Search*, 1984.

With Johnny Carson on *The Tonight Show* in 1985.

Left to right: Robin Williams, Richard Pryor, Sally Struthers, "Urban Hebrew", and Paul Mooney at a western-themed charity benefit hosted by Sally in 1981.

Backstage at the Orleans in Vegas with the king, Don Rickles, and Izzy in 2009.

Me with Julio Iglesias in Atlantic City, NJ, 1988.

Left to right: Me, George Shapiro, Ray Romano, Jason Alexander, Jerry Seinfeld, and Peter Tilden in Los Angeles, 2014.

The cast of *Everybody Loves Raymond* shooting the "Misery Loves Company" episode in season 8.

Ray and me at the Emmys, 2002.

Hanging with the master; Robin Williams, on the set of *The Crazy Ones* in 2013.

Backstage at Brad's comedy club in Vegas at the MGM, 2013. Left to right: Paul Ames, Ed Conover Jr., Chris Rock, Joe Bronzi, and Mario Joyner.

Another fun lunch with Ray. Stand-up tour in Atlanta, GA, 2009.

With good pally WJ Meade on *Gleason* set, Montreal, 2000.

Max, IsaBeall, and Hope
Las Vegas, 2014.

I know that several of you gals reading this right now may think I'm a selfish womanizer, or an unemotional man-whore, or a "squirrel trying to get a nut," as my nana used to say. But trust me, I know at least two women who feel exactly the way I do. The double standard unfortunately refers to these women as progressive, independent self-starters or lesbians. Yes, I will admit I have a fear of commitment. That fear honestly comes from the thought of never being able to touch anyone else's breasts ever again. And that's what makes me fearful. I'm committed to variety.

As we venture out for companionship in our later years, remember the three things that will break up any relationship eventually: sex, money, or smelling one's fingers during a rodeo. I strongly encourage one-night stands. You need to know right out of the gate if the one-eyed liar can dance with the taco of fury. The more time you wait to release the hounds, the more time you've wasted. If the sex sucks, you're out of Dodge with the fewest casualties.

Sex is not everything, but it becomes much larger in scope when everything else falls to shit. Another item to attach to the This Ain't Working To-Do List. It's paramount in every relationship unless you're lucky enough to be one of two people who hate sex. Highly improbable, but a home-run if this is the case. Also, nothing goes better with sex than spontaneity, and the longer you wait, the less impromptu and exciting it becomes. Women never expect older guys to be spontaneous. It's exciting to enter someone whose name is on the tip of your tongue. That's how the words "darling," "baby," and "monsignor" were created. Don't overthink it. You can always do that when you're sneaking down the stairs.

There is a reason why prostitution is the oldest and most successful business in the world.

It's not just about paying women for sex; we pay them to leave. And the older we get, the quicker we want them to leave. Without judging, questioning, or crying. That's their best attribute: hookers don't cry. Except in the movies. Or if they lie to Big Daddy. As expressed previously, the power of the pink always comes at a price, but most gals have trouble understanding why we want to pay for it.

I confessed to Izzy that I once paid a hooker for a hand job. She tried desperately, without judging(?), to understand my rationale. She appeared perplexed, so without defending or validating my actions, I tried to explain. She listened intently and responded with "But if you're going to the trouble of hiring a prostitute, why pay for something you can ultimately do yourself?"

"You don't get it," I said. "You can't have a Home Depot mentality when it comes to sex. We spend decades doing it ourselves. Sometimes we welcome the help." I suppose, being a man, I just didn't understand her question. I tried to see it from a woman's perspective, but no luck. I sputtered for a minute and thought I smelled burnt toast. It was mind-boggling to me that she found it more frivolous than unsavory. So fucking mature, in fact, that it pissed me off. So I said, "I didn't want to do it myself. That's the point. When I look down at my hand, it's not soft and supple or French-manicured. Even with my crazy imagination, when I look down there, all I see is some hairy, Hungry Jack Breakfast Man–hand, don't you understand? I'm a man, woman! We only jerk off when we're out of options!" She giggled at me the way you would at a child, kissed me on the cheek, and went to make tea. That's precisely why they're the dominant other. That's why men are the hunters and gatherers, because if we're eaten upon leaving the cave, the smarter, more insightful counterpart, doodling on the walls and waiting for Dumb-Dumb to return, can continue the species without us. And, as we know, they're very content with that possibility.

I found myself once again in the dating pool at the age of forty-five. This is where "a lot of fish in the sea" becomes "several bottom-feeders peppered with sharks possessing false teeth." The most disheartening encounter was with women my age who had decided to battle the test of time by getting "work done." I found this distorted display of vanity more of a turnoff than anything. In my opinion, it gave the younger birds an even greater advantage. What these middle-aged ladies don't seem to understand is that if we want the younger look, we'll go for someone younger. To me, there is nothing sexier than a woman who is comfortable in her own skin, literally. And the bottom line is, if you're not fooling anyone, why get the face done? The tits are easier to hide and at least leave some question in the balance. The fish lips, the pulled eyes, the frozen expression, the tight chin above the original turkey neck . . . what the hell are you doing? It's like guys who wear those ridiculous toupees. Again, if you're not fooling anyone—*which you're not*—what's the point?

I once read an article about an eighty-year-old grandmother from Vegas who asked her family for breast implants as a birthday gift. The inbred, white-trash family obliged. Nana must have looked nice with her new rock-hard tits to complement that century-old vag. Only in Vegas could you find a doc to perform such an abomination.

Ultimately, most men are fine being alone later in life, whereas women often find themselves in a frenetic race to find someone to settle down with. Take advantage of this, guys—it's one of the few times you'll be in the driver's seat. Let's look into our choices, shall we?

THE WIDOW

I should tell you from the get-go that funerals and hospitals get me horny. I've discussed this at length with my therapist, and he's concluded that it's because life never seems more fragile than when death or sickness is near. The reality check causes people with mild sexual addiction to consider mating quickly, in order to balance out the population as part of their civic duty. I also believe it has something to do with women in black. Or black nurses in white tending to our every need. Or backless gowns. Or illegal immigrants preparing a final resting place under a beautiful tree. Or a sponge bath from a stranger. It's the real "Circle of Life," without the baboon and the baby lion.

There are probably more pluses than minuses when it comes to dating a widow, compared to our other options. Unless the former husband died by the hands of the Mob, ask questions and appear concerned about her loss. But let her bring it up. If she hasn't delved into details by the time dessert arrives, she doesn't give a shit about you. Please keep in mind that widows are the most difficult to bed, especially if the loss was in the last seventy-two hours. They have double the remorse to contend with if they decide to sleep with you. The first half of their guilt comes from fear of their passed partner looking down from heaven or up from hell, neither of which is a great angle for either of you. And the second half of the guilt just comes from fucking your tired, flabby ass.

Most importantly, make sure she's not a Black Widow. If she talks about her husband's passing while pleasuring herself and shaking a rain stick, run like the wind, my friend. When a woman loses a partner through death, you may have the toughest act to follow simply because the separation was not a choice. Find out as much information as you can about the dearly departed. Like his weight, for example. The fatter, the better. If he sold Herbalife or managed a tire store, I hope you washed Area Fifty-one before picking her up, because you're most likely a lock on taking the bologna pony to tuna town. Just don't be stupid enough to ask to see a picture of him. If he ran a Fortune 500 company, had a thirty-inch waist, and skied the black diamonds, kiss her hand, say goodnight, and wish her Godspeed during her time of healing. Your chances are as dead as he is.

THE DIVORCÉE

This is by far the most complicated dating category. Because there are so many divorced women out there, go in knowing you're bound to be dealing with a mixed bag. You will need to prepare yourself for the worst and hope for the best. Depending on how her last marriage ended, she could be struggling with any number of neuroses, including insecurity, paranoia, outbursts of sobbing, rage, disbelief, abandonment issues, cat addiction, etc. Nine times out of ten, if you ask about her ex, she will spin it as "what a piece of shit he was." Adamantly agree. If by chance she takes the blame for the divorce, go shopping for a ring, but only after you're positive she's a woman. And whatever you do, don't be the prick to bad-rap your ex. It will set you back four dates and make you look like the jerk you really are.

The divorcée is in desperate need of feeling attractive. Compliment her wrists unless she has to move flesh to accurately tell the time. Be sure to mention how you like her outfit, but steer clear of jewelry, since it probably came from the ex. If out to dinner, order for her. If she's around your age, she will most likely have trouble reading the menu, so this makes you look in control as well as chivalrous. It's also a handy way to avoid paying for the surf and turf. If she dresses younger than she should, it's most likely a mess under there. If her hair is more than two colors, don't stare, but mention that her "eyes seem to change hues with the night sky" if you can't stop looking at her fucked-up coif. And ramp up the bullshit by 15 percent for every five years over fifty she happens to be.

THE NEVER WAS

This is a gal who has never walked down the aisle. There can be many reasons for this, but only two are truly commendable. Either she has invented a foolproof way of pleasuring herself, combined with an imagination that Walt Disney would envy, *or* she's loaded with dough, loves to work and travel, and has realized that most men aren't worth the small dick they rode in on. These women never bought the bullshit fairytale about the handsome prince on the white horse. They may well be in search of a black prince who's hung like a white horse, and who could blame 'em? But most likely, neither is the case.

Most "Never Was" women are batshit crazy. They'll tell you they've been engaged twice; most likely, they're the ones who proposed on both occasions. One of their parents may live next door, if not closer. They are likely to own a pair of Birkenstocks and refuse to "eat anything with a face." And something tells me, not a great blow job. If you can get your bar that low, you may find some hidden treasure: there's a very good chance she can rewire a floor lamp simply because she had to learn to do many things on her own. If you're a Jew like me who can't work a ratchet wrench, she could end up being quite cost-effective. But warn your mother beforehand that she's not one of the tribe. Because she won't be.

If you want to get this type of gal in the mood, take her to a Renaissance Faire and then go apple picking. Brag that you never had your back shaved, and drop the phrase "carbon footprint" in mixed company. But beware, these lasses usually have many secrets. Or they collect shit that most would throw away. If there's a dream catcher on her rearview mirror, she may believe the moon landing never happened. If she has a compost pile in her backyard, there will be an odor. And not from the pile. I'm sorry, but prove me wrong and I will refund your money for this book (paperback only).

One of my most heated conversations with the opposite sex was on a first/last date with a woman I was set up with at a party. She had this silent confidence that I found attractive and, for some reason, made me think she might be bisexual. Let's be honest, every guy hopes for that. Unfortunately, it ended up she was just a latent ball-buster. The argument was about whether or not it was okay for a man to receive a hand job from a paid masseuse if the man was in a relationship. I knew I wasn't going to see her again, so I felt I could be honest. I said, "Absolutely." She thought I was the seed of Satan for feeling this way and tried to turn the tables, like most females: "What if your lady was pleasured during her massage while in a relationship with you?"

"Then she got her money's worth, and it has no reflection on our relationship," I said. What I left out was: "As long as it's by another woman."

Yes, men invented hypocrisy. It's our never-ending desire to spin shit our way because our gender is notoriously greedier. (Unless the marriage crumbles.) Obviously, women are wired very differently, especially when it comes to sex.

The broad then started to spew how a real masseuse would never give a happy ending. Because that would make her a hooker. I asked, "If a hooker rubs my feet, does that make her a masseuse? Feeling good is feeling good, right?" Wrong, according to her. And, I'm sure, most gals. "But it's a full-body massage I'm paying for. Should it not include the penile region? What if I don't ask for the happy ending but she does it anyway? Am I still to blame? Who am I to tell her how to do her job?"

This reminds me of a time several years ago when I was getting a massage at a questionable establishment called

Tai Tug. After a thirty-minute rub, Madame Cougar Butterfly proceeded to ask me if I would like "a wacky-wacky." Not versed too well in "Tai," I made her repeat the offer. "You know, wacky-wacky," her hand gesture driving it home. Being a man who felt lonely and vulnerable in a strange land known as North Hollywood, I said, "Sure, why not?" in the same fashion I would answer if asked to supersize my Big Mac meal. "I be rye back!" she said with a scary wink.

So there I waited. Hanging off a table not much larger than a cutting board. Five minutes turned into fifteen and no Yoko. Was she getting dressed in something diaphanous? Or would it be the typical dragon-head-with-crotchless-panty ensemble known as "item #18"? Hopefully the latter. All of a sudden she stuck her head in the door and asked, "You finish?" The moral of my story: always tip up front.

I have always found it incredibly difficult to be faithful to one woman, and when I asked my shrink what was wrong with me, he said, "Nothing."

I asked, "Why do I do it? Fear of commitment? Lack of self-worth? Control? Insecurity?"

He replied, "Because it feels good and you enjoy variety." That was also when he told me to stop worrying, because when I hit my late forties, a lot of that urge would dissipate. Boy, he wasn't kidding. I went from watching the wiggle on the waitress's ass to watching what was on the tray. I went from pussy to pastry almost overnight. The impending devolution of thine wiener starts to take shape (or lack shape), and all of a sudden the chocolate cake is more arousing than the thirtysomething dame delivering it. More satisfying because it comes without agenda and is much cheaper in the long run. And next week, if you feel like a berry tart, the chocolate cake won't care.

The body knows when the dick is going south, but the brain is usually the last to accept it. Only when you succumb to the inevitable and stick something else in your yapper can you enjoy the bliss that is your new, quiet freedom. I guess the real key to dating later in life is not to give a shit about the outcome. Your experiences with the opposite sex (along with this book, I'm hoping), will teach you that you have very little control over your good fortune. And finding the right mate is nothing more than stone-cold luck. So learn from your mistakes and stop thinking you deserve better. You can aim high or be optimistic, but as my father used to say: "Wish in one hand and shit in the other and see which one fills up faster."

The stroke victim and the airhead.
There's someone for everyone.

16

My Body Is a Temple in Iraq

I found my first gray pubic hair on May 22, 2013—the day that part of me died.

I was eating graham crackers in bed, watching a rerun of *All in the Family,* when I dropped some crumbs on the Netherlands. Upon extracting the fragments, I noticed the fucker. Like a limp lightning bolt emerging from the valley of broken dreams, there it stood, as if to say, "Pluck me, I dare you." My girlfriend was lying next to me, and the time didn't feel opportune to yank the bastard, so I made a dash for the bathroom, because I knew I couldn't just lie there with that white barb making itself comfy in my loins.

As I stood naked, looking down at the deadened curlicue

in my reflection in the bathroom mirror, I felt surprised that it affected me so much. It was only one hair, but even more reason why it had to die. In previous years, I would pluck the grays from my temples as they would sprout, until there were just too many. Then it was the grays from my chest that I took aim at. Those, too, became unmanageable and I relented once again. But the day I saw the lone gray wolf in the lower forty-eight was the beginning of an undeniable acceptance that would not go down easy.

Then there was the reality of tweezing a dead follicle from Testicle B that got my attention a little more than, say, my nose or ear. It all made me wonder how long I could go on until I gave up, like I had with the temples and the chest. How old would I be when I looked south and admitted, "I don't know you"? Would the pain outweigh the motivation or vice versa?

And why the hell does my left ear have ten times the hair as my right ear? It makes no sense. If I moved to London, would the hair in my right ear start to balance out?

I never felt like I was in shape even in my young, thin days. At twenty-five years old, I found myself wheezing on an escalator for no reason. Maybe a fear of heights? I never worked out a day in my life, and I stand by that avoidance with pride. By middle age, I've learned something important when it comes to working out: if it ain't broke, don't fix it. In my case, that means I feel good enough without the inconvenience, boredom, and strain that come with working out. My blood pressure and heart rate are stellar, and I get enough exercise walking around parking lots looking for my car. That alone probably gets me a good two miles a week. Sure, I'd like a better shape: no love handles; more muscle definition; better stamina in the ole sack; a not-so-flabby ass. But at what price? I'm a Jew and accustomed to negotiating, and at the end of the day, I need to feel I'm getting a bargain. I just don't feel I'm getting one at Equinox for a hundred and fifty dollars a month when I could be feeding the pigeons or sexting a stranger for free.

I always had an aversion to working out, ever since my days in junior high when I was continually humiliated and ridiculed for being the slowest and weakest male in the seventh grade. Remember the Presidential Fitness Test? Kids who did so many sit-ups, pull-ups, push-ups, etc., received a lame iron-on patch and a fake certificate from the White House incumbent. The number of reps required for each calisthenic was determined by your height and weight. According to the chart, at six feet tall and 160 pounds, I should have been a redhead, married with four kids, and living in Iowa. The Presidential Fitness graph didn't go that high or even in that direction. They had to call the primate clinic to get stats on my compatibility with others. The school cafeteria worker used to feed me at arm's length. During fire drills, kids were told to "meet at Brad."

My asshole PE teacher's solution to this problem was to add ten more reps of each requirement to Antonio Palagenzo's score. Antonio Palagenzo was thirteen and had a goatee that he had to trim in between his trips to juvie. He was also the strongest kid in the San Fernando Valley and started his own gang that stole trash cans. No one really understood why, but we knew better than to question. In twelve years of public school, I was never awarded the Presidential Fitness patch. But I did buy one off of Barry Langman, just to say I had it if the topic ever came up during truth or dare. None of it really mattered. Palagenzo is at Rikers Island, and I've sold twenty-eight books. I wish I'd known that back then. It would have saved me a lot of grief and therapy.

Here's a secret: quitters finish first because they're smart enough to stop. Period. It's Madison Avenue that guilts you into "Just do it," "No pain, no gain," or "Climb it because it's there" idiocy. No pain? Guess what? No doctor, no ointment, no piss-tasting Gatorade. And no money for the corporations that make this crap to fix our bodies because we're attempting shit we shouldn't be doing. How many people do you know who ski? Out of those people, how many should not? Eighty percent? More like 90. And why do they ski? Because their ego convinces them they can. There's a reason why urgent care is at the bottom of the hill and not at the top.

Jim Fixx, the health and fitness guru and successful author most famous for his running accomplishments and unprecedented endurance, died from running. It wasn't enough that he was already in great shape and the spokesman for Grape-Nuts. He had to keep proving it by running some more until his friggin' heart imploded on lap 207. Why? For what?

Richard Simmons made $50 million—you heard me, $50 million—with his frightening "Sweating to the Oldies" crap and his Dial-A-Meal propaganda. You think he's in shape? This guy sweats more when he has to strap on his heels because he's late for a parade. You don't get a gut like that from "taking it to the limit," Home Fry.

I once had Jack LaLanne, the Godfather of Fit, in the front row at one of my shows. He looked half-dead in that scary baby-blue jumpsuit, like an extra from "Thriller," with the family cat masquerading as his hair. I told him that his blood tested positive for dust and that I read his diary from the Civil War. Feeling attacked, he jumped up from his chair and proceeded to tell me, "I may be eighty-three, but I can still touch my toes!" I told him, "Yeah, but it doesn't count if you do it with your balls." And that's my point, ladies and gentlemen. You age anyway. Gravity and the hands of time have a deathgrip on your prostate, so why the rippled biceps? Who are they for, Gunther? The pink, that's who. Have you learned nothing?

Good genetics play a big part in all of this. Even though cancer has killed more people in my family than one can imagine, my ticker might as well be Swiss-made. As far as my grille, I stay on it like a second job because the family genes were not so kind to the Chiclets. My zadie, who by the way called me a schmuck on his deathbed before drifting off to wherever we go, had dentures by age thirty-five. He never brushed a day in his life and kept the chompers in a cup at night, fizzing away. As kids, my cousin Darren and I used to sneak into Zadie's bathroom in Oxnard when we visited and marvel that he could actually take his teeth out of his head. When Zadie arrived at Ellis Island from Poland in 1926, he was twenty-three. An immigration officer stamped his papers and four teeth fell out. He never looked back.

My father had horrible teeth as well, rest his soul. He was a child of poverty, and dental care was a luxury. His teeth were as loose as a girl in a prom dress. He once took me to a petting zoo, and the owner gave him a carrot and a cube of sugar.

I had a ton of dental care as a kid, including braces. Now my teeth are starting to succumb to my lineage. I recently was told by my dentist that my gums are receding because I brushed too hard and too often in my younger years. He also told me that I take my floss too deep. Huh? I felt like bitch-slapping the old doc. Who does he think is at fault for giving me that advice? My gums are retreating like the Dutch army, and I have a ton of root showing from brushing too often and flossing too well. My pearls could end up like Steve Buscemi's, a hundred grand later. But Zadie's smile? Like a pearl necklace on Pamela Anderson. The kind she never paid for but definitely deserved.

17

No Scales in Heaven

Art and wine age well, so why the hell can't we? And I don't mean "preserve" well. Who gives a shit how you look? I'm talking about pulling out the stops and trying to find your balls of yesteryear, when they were a tad higher and things were attempted with less fear. I've spent middle age in search of who the hell I really am, settling on the philosophy that "what you see is what you get, Jack." That freedom becomes possible only with a great deal of maturity, experience, and denial. Or when we just plain burn out from pretending to be that guy we never were. You will get to that last hole on that belt you bought in 2002, so prepare accordingly.

As we know by now, the theme of this book can be

summed up in one word: don't buy the hype. Okay, that's four words. If your doctor tells you to lose weight, look at *all* the variables involved in that advice. For starters, how fat is he or she? My doctor happens to be fifty pounds overweight. If he's armed with the best medical information, what's *his* story? And exactly how am I supposed to lose the weight? What do I have to give up? What's in it for me if I conform? Is the dread of losing late-night ice cream really going to outweigh the six pounds I lose by Christmas, only to put it on again because if I don't shove my mouth full of holiday goose, I might tell the family how I feel about them?

How many minutes of jogging must I endure to lose this weight, Doctor? What if three men in my family died of heart attacks before the age of fifty? Can I factor that in and say I'm not changing squat because the odds are stacked against me anyway? Yes. Yes, I believe I can. Or, in the words of the great Jewish philosopher: "Damn straight."

If it's true that we are what we eat, then it's safe to say, "We shit what we were." So it's a push. It's all good. The oldest person I ever knew was my ex-wife's grandmother. She lived to be a ripe 102 years old. Being gentile and upbeat, I'm sure, had a lot to do with it. The woman ate like she was going to the electric chair. I thought the warden was going to come in any minute and blindfold her. She ate pork every day and loved her Arby's roast beef sandwiches (which has to be the furthest thing from roast beef known to man). She downed those suckers like they were mints. She loved her sherry, had a liking for fudge and the word "negro," and scarfed three bratwursts and a quart of Guinness at an Octoberfest on her ninety-fifth birthday. Then she proceeded to drive home. Even the Asians pulled over.

My point is, it's not the food that kills you. It's your genetics, stress, and DNA. And luck of the draw. In other words, you have zero control over it. Eat right, and a bad ticker is a bad ticker. Bathe in biscuits and gravy until your aorta emerges from your left nipple, and you're fine as long as your grandpoppy was a miner and your mother worked on engines during her third trimester. Chances are you'll hit seventy even if you abuse the shit out of yourself (see: the Rolling Stones).

And so be it. You never hear anyone say, "Ohhh, if I could just relive my seventies and have that stroke at the mall again. Waking up facedown in front of Pottery Barn, mumbling the name of my cat while a Mexican kid ate a churro over my forehead as the paramedics ripped open my shirt like a Hong Kong parasol . . . good times!" Here's what I suggest: throw a few Lipitors into the piehole and start up the hibachi. Cornbread's on me.

Oh, and don't let some quack tell you there's a good cholesterol and a bad one. They're either both good or both bad. And what's the difference? I wish I had a dollar for every vegetarian I met who outweighed me by seventy-five pounds. I can hear the heifers whining as I write this: "I only eat vegetables." I'm thinking: *so do elephants.* You're fat and you're not fooling anyone. If you want to spin it your way, be honest and tell everyone you're hiding refugees in your ass until the Germans blow through town. Or don't. Either way, take it all with a grain of salt. Or a handful of popcorn and more salt. With some of that fake friggin' movie theater butter that I love—so bad for you that you now have to put it on yourself. The theater will no longer be liable for administering something that lethal to the pulmonary system. But remember: free refills.

I've never met a happy vegetarian. Never. I've met content ones. I've never seen one who looks relatively healthy, either. They may be on the inside, but the outside is gasping for gristle. When I dine with one, I know they want a bite of my burger. I see it in their little beady protein-deficient eyes. They shun my steak and judge my chicken as their bony yellow mitt reaches for a snow pea with the salad fork 'cause the bigger fork is too heavy.

I'm frustrated with them because they are the kink in the food chain. I understand they love animals. So do I, and I promise not to eat my pets. Or the neighbor's. Or even the horse I dropped nine hundred dollars on at Santa Anita. But I'm going to put the hurt on a cow. I understand they're cute and didn't do anything wrong and have the eyelashes of a stripper, but I'm sorry. They're slow and stand by the highway for a reason. Easy access to market. They're begging for it. And I prefer my steak crazy-rare. Take the cow, wipe its ass, and walk it through a warm room, and I'm happy. Then throw some béarnaise and crab on it. Pigs are cute when they're under five pounds. After that, all bets are off because, as we know, bacon is the Lord's candy.

I feel it's my duty as an American to help thin out the herd. But being that this American is of Jewish descent (though not enough of a Jew to avoid pork), I like to get a middleman to do the dirty work for me. In other words, if I had to kill the beast myself, I would probably become a vegetarian by proxy. That's why I can't hunt. But I can eat.

And please don't be one of these douchey culinary spin doctors who are not animal activists per se but come up with convenient ways to explain how their lust for carnage is more humane. Like free-range chicken. "They're treated better than other chickens." Are you fuckin' kidding me? They're treated much worse. Mentally tortured, in fact. Why? Because they're *free-range*. They're made to believe they're free because they're "set free." Able to roam. Freely. On the range. But it's a terrible lie. At least the birds in their small cages understand their true fate. "Free-range" is Latin for "ten-minute head start" and nothing more. Corn-fed steer? Not even worth discussing.

I also recently learned about "sustainable salmon." Apparently, it's much more humane to eat than Chicken of the Sea or Alaskan king crab. Sustainable salmon are caught only after they have bred and are on their way downstream from their one-night stand. Salmon die after breeding, so the more humane fisherman figured, let's kill them before they die and convince you stupid diners these guys were on their way to death anyway and you'll feel less guilty. Why? Because you must believe there are clairvoyant fisherman out there who will be able to detect which fish screwed the night before. Are they wearing evening attire (the swim of shame) during the day on their way downstream? Smoking that afterglow ciggy? Avoiding all the texts on their phone the next day, etc.?

Quick question, since we're stuck on food: if the crab in the salad isn't real, what the fuck is it? Imitation crab, I get it, but that doesn't answer the question. Who's impersonating the crab? What species is it? It's still a kind of seafood, I'm guessing, but what, exactly? When it's imitation chicken, it's usually tofu or some shit pounded together with grain, veggies, and I don't know what else. But the fake crab must be a sea creature, too. Just tell us what it is! They've got us eating sea urchin now—I'm sure it ain't worse than that. Is it hermit crab? I can take it, just come clean.

The fanatical vegans also avoid honey and leather (two things I can't run out of in my bedroom). I didn't know bees were smoke-stunned so honey makers could collect the honey—I really didn't. Don't care, either. One could argue that they kind of deserve it after stinging ninety million people yearly worldwide.

And there are those who won't wear leather. They don't

seem to understand the cow is already dead because we needed the ribeyes, but whatever. I think they're just cheap bastards who need an excuse to buy a vinyl belt. But of course someone figured out a way to cash in on the humane as well. Stella McCartney, Paul McCartney's daughter—someone who really needs the dough—has her own designer line of vegan-synthetic accessories. Beautiful purses, not made of leather, starting at a couple grand apiece. They're plastic. As in really cheap. Twice as much as leather. I don't get it. I thought all you needed was love.

Bottom line: no one has any idea what's good for us and what's not. And by the time they figure it out, we'll already be blown to bits by a third-world country that we supported for years, only to find out their donkeys were used as suicide livestock. Look it up, it happened. And if the secret can be found in nature, why is everyone waiting in line to get a prescription filled? Take the acai berry, for instance, or whatever that new tiny fruit is that they discovered in South America that is supposedly the new cure-all, the key to the fountain of youth. It's the one Oprah eats before sending Stedman off to bed in the guesthouse so she and Gayle can play Rosa Parks and the Milkmaid. (I may have just blown my chances of getting into Oprah's Book Club, but a man is allowed to dream.)

I once heard a scientist on the news say: "The monkeys in the rainforest have been eating these purple berries for years . . ." This just in: Jane Goodall called, and it's time to get thine head out of thine ass. Or rent *Gorillas in the Mist* and play it backward. Those primates she's referring to live to be thirty-five, on average. If the berry is really that great, maybe the monkeys would choose to eat it over the mites they pick off their buddy's anus. Just because some wacko with access to a Bunsen burner and a PhD in horticulture says it's the magical fruit of tomorrow, everyone's tripping over themselves at Trader Joe's to get a bottle. You ever see the folks who live in the rain forest? Not exactly the picture of health. The reality is, you can eat right your whole life and your colon can still end up more twisted than Courtney Love.

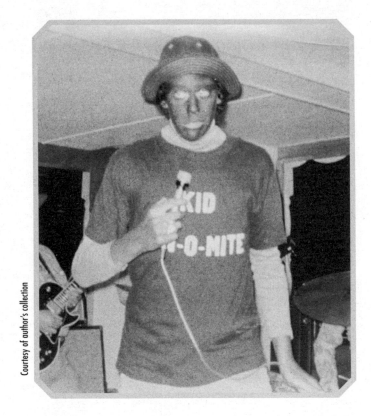

My fully committed Jimmie Walker impression at the Funk Bar Mitzvah, 1975.

18

Embrace Your Stereotype

If you haven't noticed, I'm not very politically correct, nor do I have a very useful filter. I call it like I see it, and I welcome the world to do the same (unless you're Rush Limbaugh).

I feel that stereotypes exist because they are factual and authentic in nature at least 90 percent of the time. Stereotypes usually come from traditions and habits that are innocently passed down or inherited, and for that reason alone, we need to learn to embrace them. They also come from jokes shared at cocktail parties or holiday suppers from one generation to the next, thus continuing the cycle in a more palatable manner. And since my humor falls on the more racial end of the spectrum, I appreciate this opportunity to help you learn to take yourself and others more lightly.

Is it racist to ask my black friend where I should go in New Orleans for soul food? Is it racist if my Armenian friend asks me whether I can recommend any Jewish friends selling diamonds downtown? Is it wrong if I ask my Irish buddy for a good place in Boston to drink beer and throw darts? Am I being stereotypical or racist? Or are these just questions posed to people who know what the fuck I'm talking about? Should I go up to an East Indian and ask him where the best bagels are in Montreal? Does that make everyone feel more comfortable? Will the bagel be great? I think not. But let him fix my computer and I'll be one happy camper.

Stereotypes are purely mathematical statistics. There is a very good chance that most African-American men I come across will have a larger penis than I do. Not all. But most. As in 99 percent most. And because of the law of statistics, my memory of high school gym class, and my smallish, rabbi-ravaged member, I will not ask the ones I'm in doubt of to prove it. I wouldn't even ask them to take out just enough to win. I will believe them blindly. Because to win, you must play the odds.

I have a dear black friend, who will remain nameless, who literally had to get *re*circumcised at age eighteen. Are you fucking listening? RECIRCUMSIZED. As in "My dick outgrew its skin," people. Was his schlong reptilian? No, of course not. It was African-American. And God bless him, because I can't imagine having that procedure done at eighteen years of age. That said, I would go through the agony if my outcome were equivalent to what he started with. This particular friend is also an amazing swimmer, so there goes my stereotypical theory on that. In my defense, I believe he uses his massive wang as a body snorkel in order to help his amphibian tendencies. Again, just a guess.

Speaking of wangs, Asians are smart. If I needed a student to cheat off of in school, I tended to sit next to Lily Fujikawa instead of Domino Lopez. Doesn't mean Domino isn't as bright as Lily, but being a born gambler, I gotta go with Fujikawa in chemistry class. Don't get me wrong, Lopez gets the nod if I can't figure out why my car won't start. Ironically, neither does his, and what's up with that? They're often wonderful mechanics, but their shit never runs. You would think the one thing they've learned from the border police is: "I need a ride that works."

Is it racist to say that you never see an Asian guy in porn, or is it a bloody fact? Asians are also notoriously terrible drivers. There's never been one to win the Indy 500. That's just the way it is, and my good friend Wayne, who is Chinese, explained it to me brilliantly. He put us both in front of a mirror and said: "Look at my eyes. They're obviously a different shape than yours in a way that would decrease my peripheral vision. Now try squinting your eyes to the point where you can still see, but in line with the size of my eye opening. See?

Pretty shitty." So next time you're cut off by an Asian on the highway, take this into consideration before using a slur that's perhaps racist yet accurate. A stereotypical, factual slur may suffice, such as: "That fuckin' high achiever just cut me off! Friggin' 4.0 nuclear motherfucker." See the difference? Racist? Not really. Insightful and resourceful? Absolutely.

"Know your customer" is what my father the salesman always taught me.

White Men Can't Jump was the title of a very successful movie. It's also a known fact, in general. If I made a movie called *Black Guys Can Really Jump,* does that make me a racist? What if the movie depicted only fat white people looking straight up into the sky, wearing LeBron jerseys and eating hot dogs, like they usually do? Does that mean "I hate whitey"? My point is, white men can indeed jump. Especially when being scared by a black man. This has happened to me on several occasions. Mostly in Miami. (Wait, those were Cubans.)

If I say 70 percent of professional football players are black, is that a racial remark? Or simply a fact—that many African-American people are gifted in sports. And music. And in being able to wear the color magenta. Martin Luther King Jr. Day is a very worthy holiday for recognizing one of the most courageous and insightful Americans who ever lived. But wouldn't it make more sense to have a day when jobs are *given* to African-Americans instead of something they don't need, like another day off?

My people, the Jews, are known for their frugality or cheapness. Not all, but in general. Oh, and their big noses. I happen to spend money like I'm allergic to it, and my nose has been compared to Scarlett Johansson's, but that's me. I'm sure there are many Jews who are generous. But not in general. I know three. Some historians say it may have something to do with the atrocities that my people had to endure when they were robbed of their belongings as well as their lives. Did this become an unfortunate stereotype rooted in brutal experiences and fact? Or is it that my people are smart enough to know you don't tip on tax and liquor?

Speaking of liquor, the Native Americans shared in a similar plight, but probably not as many because they were able to get away on horseback. We didn't have that advantage. If you see a Jew with a horse, he just won the Kentucky Derby. Plus, the Indians now have their own casinos, are allowed to hit on soft seventeen, and don't have to pay taxes, so I'm assuming they'll stop bitching. My people, not so much.

The Asians were treated like shit for a long time as well, but we've all gotten used to paying eleven dollars for a bowl of rice, so now we're even. But I'm not living down the Pearl Harbor bullshit because I love Hawaii.

How about the poor Italians who found it difficult to purchase weapons upon leaving Ellis Island and now find themselves controlling some of the best hookers and drugs in the free world? This is the land of opportunity, and we can't lose our sense of humor while dissecting it.

There's a reason why my grandfather changed his name from Cohen to Colton upon coming to the United States from Poland. The Polack jokes were tough enough, so maybe the Jew thing would go under the radar? Hardly. His nose was enormous.

Most importantly, let's learn from our stereotypes. They are chock-full of wonderful information.

Attention, my African-American brothers: enough with the giant gold necklaces. Less is more, but remember your history. You shouldn't be wearing chains, right? Or anything cotton. But stick with the Confederate flag toilet paper.

Attention, my Asian brothers and sisters, one word: orthodontia. You gotta trust me and keep the teeth straight. Way too much other shit for us to pick on. And when you can, try to appear surprised instead of sleepy—fight the feeling and stay in the moment. Oh, and try to laugh once a month. Helps move around bok choy in tummy.

Attention, White Trash: don't even worry about orthodontia; just having any teeth at all would help. More than four would be delightful. And take down your fuckin' Christmas lights before Memorial Day. And get over the breakup of the Little River Band. If you must chew tobacco, please do it only while wearing your sheeted hood, because no one wants to see that. I feel your angst to compete at the flea markets, but this just in: no one wants your old shit.

Attention, Latinos, Mexican-Americans, and All-Around Help: please get someone to read this to you. Stop parking on your lawn. There's a driveway two feet away. The grass hates it, not to mention the pink plastic flamingo. Also, we don't want to buy your fruit next to the freeway. It's too tricky for a thousand reasons. We have the same shit at the market. Oranges aren't that hard to get. You're really not cutting out the middleman, you're just stealing from the middleman by trying to sell it directly to whitey. Instead of trying to sell us shit, how about returning what you stole? And don't take offense to this, please. If I didn't believe in you, I wouldn't leave my children in your care.

Attention, fellow Jews: it's just food. Slow the fuck down. The sandwich was originally designed to fit *inside* your mouth. Save some for the next guy. And not everything has to be a fuckin' bargain. Milk is a certain price per gallon, period. Put away the Magic Marker and quit trying to mess with the expiration date. And quit bitching about being forced to build the pyramids. You owned the land, and who knows better than us: if you want something done right, you have to do it yourself.

Attention, Irish folk: attempt to read this only after your hangover subsides. And after you're done apologizing to your woman for the shiner you gave her last night that you don't remember. Oh, and call your brother, the cop or fireman. If your cholesterol isn't over 315, you're not actually Irish, so demand a DNA test from Pappy.

Attention, Italians: you're not all in the Mob, so stop acting like it. And quit grabbing your crotch. The blacks have a reason, you don't. And don't keep taking your laundry to your mama's so you can leave with her leftovers. The cord is so long, you could hang five snitches from it. Cut her loose.

I could go on, but I can only read so much hate mail. Remember, we're all perfectly flawed and ethnically diverse—but I digress. A racial joke beats lobbing a bomb over a border any day. Oh, and the Arabs? This book ain't big enough. Who ordered goat?

19

Mental Wellness

People rarely change. Especially since the banning of electric shock treatment. I realize in an earlier chapter, I mentioned that people *do* change. But at our core, we are who we are. Hence, the Three Strikes Law. If doing fifteen years in the big house by day and moonlighting as someone's bitch at night doesn't set you straight, I have a feeling that Dr. Phil lecturing you on anger management in that hayseedy Southern-redneck drawl ain't gonna do it, either. Our tastes and habits change, especially considering we're the most fickle species on the planet. But real self-change is a rarity.

What we do know is: few people change, most repeat, and all lie. So what's the point?

The experts don't have the answers; they have hype combined with charisma, financial backing, and brilliant salesmanship. Even Dr. Oz lied to me and the world about shedding ten pounds in five days. Is there no shame?

Take my fellow giant, the charming Tony Robbins, with that huge smile like the entrance to a fun house. I learned a long time ago that when someone smiles continually, he either has just let one rip or someone's about to take a slug. I'm sure he means well, but I'm not ready to burn a three-day weekend learning about "brotherhood," followed by a walk on hot coals. You want to learn something useful? Have the life coach teach you how to walk on eggshells so you can deal with your old lady after you return from that three-day bachelor party in Cabo. "I did it! I walked on coals! I made it through the rain!" Yeah, so did Manilow, and now he's banished to life in Vegas.

The key is to realize that at the end of the day, you're most likely very fucked up. If you think I'm not talking about you, you're fucked up beyond repair with more baggage than a Carnival cruise. You have to stop bullshitting yourself *now*. Quit the charade and stop trying to be someone you're not. Save time and money and burn those skinny jeans.

I had to break down last year and buy the old-man thunder-bags also known as "dad jeans." The unfortunate fact revolving around my high taste in clothes is that I'm usually limited to the shit they sell at those Big 'N' Tall

bull-tiques, such as the store I affectionately refer to as
Big Fat Fucks. For years I've tried to convince those store-
owners not to put their crappy threads in the damn windows. It helps no one whatsoever. Do we really need to see
a size 68XXXL beige suit behind glass while at a stoplight?
You have to make a right turn to see how they finished
the shoulders. Does a 450-pound man need a sleeveless
sweater-vest? Or does he need a shirt just small enough
that it keeps him from raising a fork to his mouth? How
about a belt that automatically closes another inch every
sixty days, whether you want it to or not? And shouldn't
pastel colors be outlawed for anyone over six-four? Or
should we really walk around looking like giant scoops of
sherbet? Why not a helmet built into a nice fez or fedora
for when we hit our head every time we're sneaking out of
Home Town Buffet? How about a pair of size-fifteen shoes
that don't look like they should come with a pair of bolts
for your neck? And why do they make shoes that large in
white? "Look at me! I'm a giant nurse!" What the hell? Put
this shit in front of a mirror before slapping it on the backs
of random pituitary cases.

Last time I was at Big Fat Fucks, they asked if I would
sign a picture that they could put on their Wall of Fame,
alongside the likes of Pavarotti, Orson Welles, John Candy,
the actor who played Jaws in that Bond film, Christopher
Hewett (Mr. Belvedere), and others whose hearts had imploded while they attempted to tie their shoes. I told them

I was only a burrito away from deserving that induction, and they would receive a photo within the next hundred pounds.

If you have been lucky enough to dodge the men in the white coats, your only saving grace is to let those around you, especially potential dates/business partners/prosecutors, know how fucked up you really are. I feel that telling it like it is becomes a turn-on for most of the opposite (or same) sex because few do it. And we all love rooting for the underdog, so why not make that dog you?

Your best shot in life is finding someone as messed up as you are or worse. Yes, water seeks its own level, but so does vomit. Lower the bar and get laid more. And forget the notion that opposites attract. They distract. Learn from the jungle. You may see a monkey in a tree looking down at a tiger, thinking, *I'd like to fuck me that cat,* but he doesn't act on it. Even the stupid monkey knows that if he plays it out with kitty, he's gonna end up one dickless chimp. That's why you never see a warthog hanging with a dingo unless Disney's behind it.

When it comes to relationships, my father always told me: "The best relationships are a blending of neuroses." Truly a marvelous evaluation of the human condition. Though, as I mentioned earlier, he was married six times, which he said proved his point. He wasn't much of a blender, but he owned five of them—all wedding gifts.

People who are always looking to better themselves are

generally very annoying. Everyone looking on knows these people have no chance of changing because they're incapable of it. If you worked on bettering yourself twenty-four hours a day, the difference would be negligible at best, while you appeared desperate to the world. Fucked-up people need to come out. Transparency as a society is our only hope.

Paul Mobley

"Does this dog make my penis look bigger?"

20

Bad Decisions
With Good Intentions

Bad decision #1: trying desperately to hold on to your youth.

If you're in your mid-forties or older, you're not allowed to get a tattoo or an earring if you don't already have one, understand? I'm speaking mostly to the men. It's one thing to yearn for your youth, but I can't allow you to look like a douche while you hold on to it with a death grip. If you have tats and earrings, you better be a recognizable rock star or belong to a motorcycle gang. It's no different than seeing a sixty-year-old broad in Daisy Dukes and a tube top. She's the only one who enjoys that, not us. It's desperate and unattractive. (Note: I'm writing this wearing my dad jeans, a T-shirt with a duck on it, and warm slippers—join me here on the older side of denial and don't look back. Or do what you want and come off as a sad, insecure imbecile who's praying that Blue Oyster Cult reunites.)

Also, attention, any asshole over twenty-three who rides a skateboard: you're affecting our reputation as a species that walks upright. Get a fuckin' clue. If your skateboard loses a ball bearing, what's your option? Your little sister's Big Wheel? Unless you're cruising for kids, buy a friggin' car, for crying out loud. You can get one on Craigslist for two grand (the same place you bought that futon for your room in Mom's basement). If you think you look cool, buy a full-length mirror and reevaluate . . . pre–bong hit. Grow up. It's more fun to be a big kid. If you're worried about looking cool, how about getting a job? That's kind of cool.

Not to sound like an old fart, but I also really need you younger kids to think long and hard about getting tattoos. They're forever. When you're in your twenties, you have no idea what forever is, but think twice before getting that red hibiscus flower inked over your taint or the Tasmanian Devil forty-five degrees south of your left nut. And if you think they were painful to apply, the removal is ten times more painful. I don't know this firsthand, but I have friends who are ex-cons, and we all know they don't lie.

To the kids who get piercings in their noses, tongues, lips, eyelids, labia, not to mention the bread plates stretched into the lobes of rebellious teens from the Valley who think they have a spiritual connection to the people of Uganda, I say: "Next!" Please, save something for Halloween. Yes, I believe in self-expression and thinking differently and with authenticity, but some of this shit becomes an addiction and a form of self-mutilation. If you have a bone in your nose, saucers in your ears, and a tribal tattoo on your neck, you better have some great dance moves around a huge kettle as you prepare to eat a missionary. If not, stay the hell out of the show, light-skinned Makumba.

Most of this book is aimed at people of my generation, but for any youngsters reading, please set your feelings of invincibility aside for a moment. We age, and that means YOU WILL, TOO. So ladies, know that the cute little scorpion tattoo you have on your perky titty is sexy today, but when you're seventy, it's gonna look like a lobster hanging by a claw. And the last thing the kiddies need to see at Thanksgiving is Grandma's lobster dipping into the yams. Nor do they need the pressure of getting your shiny nipple ring away from the kitten. It's the holidays, for Christ's sake.

Now I need to address the tattoo the ladies get right above their bunghole, also known as the "tramp stamp." First of all, being right above your crack, it's close to impossible to see without a mirror, correct? Unless you're an owl with 180-degree head-turning capability. I knew one girl who had a dragonfly and a butterfly right above the Chat-tahoochee Canal. Guess what? Not that attractive. I don't know about you, but I'm not big on seeing flies of any kind emanating from that area. Dated a "dancer" for two hours who had a skull and crossbones in the same place. Lovely. Nothing better than feeling like you're fucking a pirate or a poisonous substance.

Here's a thought: get a tattoo for us guys to enjoy, since we're the ones back there trying to get you back to the barn. Something motivating like, I don't know, a cheeseburger, or maybe a tattoo of your sister who'd we really rather bang. Or maybe I'm just jealous because I don't have the cojones to endure the pain of getting some ink on my rumply ass or lack-of-bicep.

Oh, and a note to my African-American brothers and sisters: most tattoos are a waste of your time. They just end up putting extra pressure on your friends to try and figure out what it is you've got on there. How can I say this without being offensive? Because as we know, that's not my thing . . . but it's hard as shit to see. That's why Mike Tyson said, "Fuck it. It goes on my face." Save us all the trouble or use Wite-Out.

We must face the truth and move along, people. And not on a skateboard, wearing an earring, and sporting a snake tat-too. Because it's been done way too much, and you're better than that. And people *are* pointing and laughing, you just can't hear it over the carny music that continually plays inside your head. Be yourself. Shit, maybe that *is* being yourself . . . if so, I don't know what to tell ya.

Just use your common sense, okay? Ask yourself, "Will this make me look like a douche?" "Am I too old for this bracelet?" "Should I shave the beatnik patch of hair off my four chins?" "Should my car be red if I'm not Persian?" "Is it better to have my hammertoe fixed before buying new sandals?" "Is it okay for my necklace to have a Jewish star *and* a crucifix?" "If I text a picture of my penis, can I keep my shirt on?" Only you know these answers, and I trust you.

Bad decision #2: filling the void with too many pets.

One of the nice things about growing older is you can have as many pets as you want. But as with cookies, your parents were right: there is such a thing as too many. Being deprived of this privilege as a kid, I more than made up for it in my adult life. What I love the most about dogs is that, unlike people, they are exactly the same every day. As predictable as a sunrise or a cold sore on picture day. Also, unlike people, they shit, piss, and puke on various items that happen to be nowhere near a toilet. Not to mention the incessant licking of their baggage in front of dinner guests. So why the hell did I acquire four?

My herd is comprised of the following: I have a blue-tick coonhound named Betty who was a rescue and hiding among a group of various Labradors up for adoption. My son, Max, picked her out of the doggy lineup. Next is Chester, the West Highland terrier. He was a gift from the ex-wife in exchange for the house, the cars, my dignity, etc. Then I have Lucy, a twelve-year-old yellow Lab who is showing signs of old age and suffering from dog-mentia: barking continually at imaginary objects. Last is Bernice, a Bernese mountain dog, a breed known for pulling small wagons in the Alps. Bernice is practically maimed from a rare neurological disorder, thanks to the puppy mills that sell to high-end pet stores, so there will be no pulling of anything. She wears a harness with a handle so we can lift her up when she needs help. My daughter, Hope, calls her "Lunchbox." She's not in pain, just a big pain in the ass who has to be lifted and pushed to go anywhere. Just imagine Larry Flynt if he were a dog.

The thing that gets me most crazy about Bernice is that she eats her own shit. I'm a huge animal lover, but when I witness this, I consider burning my PETA hoodie and ordering veal. I've tried for years to convince her to stop. Yelling, offering cookies and bones instead of her feces, pleading with embarrassment when she displays this habit while company is over, all to no avail. I took her to my trusted veterinarian, Dr. Lisa, and said, "Bernice eats her own shit, and I'm losing friends. What can you do?"

The good doctor replied, "Brad, this is very common in

the canine world. What you need to do is put something on the shit to make it taste bad." (Please reread the last line and let me know if you blanked like I did.)

"What? Put something on the shit *to make it taste bad*?" I retorted. "What on God's green earth can I possibly put on shit to make it taste worse than *shit*? You're losing me, Doc."

She said, "Do you have any Tabasco around the house?"

"I'm sure I do somewhere. I mean, I'm no Emeril, but I can tell you I don't think it tastes worse than shit."

"Listen to me. When the dog is done pooping, immediately take the Tabasco and pour some right onto the crap. She won't eat it again after that. Guaranteed." Now, there's the paranoid part of me that thinks I'm being punk'd and this is going to end up on a blooper show. But she is a doctor, so she must know what she's talking about.

Cut to six-thirty the next morning. I was standing in my robe in the backyard, sprinkling my dog's steaming pile of shit with a newly opened bottle of Tabasco. I was staring at Bernice like "Don't you make a liar out of Dr. Lisa, you hear me?"

And the dog was looking at me wagging her tail and, I swear, actually smiling as if to say, "You are the best owner ever! I can't believe you're seasoning my shit! No wonder we're best friends! Can't wait to tell the cat."

In the end, the dog ate her crap faster than she's ever eaten anything in her life. I'm not proud to say I wanted to hit her with the Tabasco bottle, but it's rather tiny and wouldn't do much to a hundred-pound dog who's already crippled. Plus, the neighbor was watching.

When I shared this fiasco with my buddies during a poker game, one of them piped up and said, "Don't use Tabasco, man. You're supposed to use pineapple. Everyone knows it's pineapple."

"Do they, Leonard?" I asked. "Pineapple will keep them from eating shit, you say?"

"Yep. Worked with my Yorkie. And they say dogs that eat shit are vitamin-deficient."

"And what better place to find nutrients and vitamins than in one's shit, right?" I mumbled.

"Try the pineapple, Brad. Thank me later."

I never did try putting pineapple on the dog shit. I figured if the hot sauce didn't blow off the deal, a sweet Hawaiian fruit wouldn't turn the bitch around, either. And I wasn't willing to risk it. Because I love pineapple. And I want to keep it that way.

I just have to close with one last note about the so-called designer dog breeds that have hit the market over the last several years, each costing literally thousands of dollars. The Puggle, Labradoodle, Yorkalier, and so on. Guess what? They're just mutts, people. The neighbor's German shepherd getting out and having its way with the Jones's bulldog does not make it okay to sell the offspring, known as Gerbulls, for twenty-five hundred each. If a poodle is fucked by a Rottweiler, I think a discount and possibly a lawsuit are in order, not an opportunity to drop three grand on a species that wasn't meant to evolve. Why are the mutts at the pound free and the others cost a fortune? And why stop here? Let's really bastardize the genetic relevance of what's acceptable. How about hooking up a harbor seal with a Chihuahua while we're at it? Imagine the bark on that pup. Plus, they can swim back to the border where they originated.

Bad decision #3: overcompensating with wheels.

The classic bad midlife-crisis decision inevitably involves a vehicle. I firmly believe that expensive sports cars would not cost nearly as much if guys didn't buy them to get laid. Most guys in a Ferrari have no right to be in one. Including me. Been there, done that.

I remember a few years back, when my midlife crisis was in full swing, I decided to drop close to three hundred grand on a gorgeous yellow Ferrari 360 Modena. I knew nothing about that car, but I knew my penis would be thrilled with the purchase. I showed up with my cousin Darren at a luxury automobile agency in Beverly Hills and inquired about a test drive. Most guys would get laughed out of the showroom, but television is a powerful thing, and the sales manager proceeded to move the 360 from the center of the showroom to Wilshire Boulevard. It took me three attempts to physically get into the car. Like all sports cars, it wasn't designed for a giant. The car salesman, being a whore like they always are, convinced me he knew a guy in the Valley who could put the seat rails back and get me another two inches of legroom. "We did that for Shaq," gloated the greaseball.

The extra legroom wouldn't have mattered, since I hit my melon hard trying to enter the cockpit. As I grabbed my left leg to pull it into the car, my shoe popped off and got stuck under the clutch. I proceeded to take the other shoe off. The manager photocopied my license, gave me a three-minute tutorial, then Darren and I were off. It was a manual transmission, which I always wanted in a sports car because that was "real driving." The problem was, my last stick-shift experience was in my first car, back in 1976, and that was my dad's '72 Pinto Runabout. This Ferrari transmission was just not as forgiving.

As I hit 75 mph in first gear, I noticed a lot of white smoke accompanying my jerky shifting. This particular model had the glass covering the engine compartment directly behind the driver seat. Now the smell of smoke was oddly creeping into our area. *What a piece of crap,* I thought. *What new car smokes like this?* Afraid of blowing up, we raced back to the dealership, where we were met by a very irate sales manager and an Italian-speaking Ferrari technician. The interior was full of smoke. Seems I had burned out the clutch. "That's impossible!" said I, the idiot. I was looking at a nine-thousand-dollar repair. In my dire compulsivity, I convinced him to write off the repair if I bought the car in an automatic model. He, of course, obliged.

"But you can't even fit in it," said my practical cousin.

"Relax. Don't confuse me with logic," I uttered, and drove home in the automatic. I will not lie, it was pretty amazing. Except for the fact that my left leg fell asleep after three miles, and I was afraid to get out of the car in that condition; we've all had to walk with a sleeping leg at one time or another, and it's never pretty. Especially after exiting an Italian sports car.

I had never wanted to be five-ten more in my life than the day I took the Modena to a racetrack in Lancaster to partake in a driving school where owners of every car imaginable could show up and go out on the track with a professional driver. The idea was the pro would give you a crash course on driving for about thirty minutes as he drove your car, and then you would drive him around for thirty minutes while he critiqued your technique. After that, you were on your own for the rest of the day while you practiced what you had learned. At least that's what it said in the brochure.

I met Dirk, the driver, in his silver flame-retardant jumpsuit. He told me to get a helmet from the race shop and meet him on the track. I have a large head, and they had only one XXL left. I managed to squeeze it on, but unfortunately, it made me over seven fuckin' feet tall. This posed an even bigger problem: there was literally no way for me to fit into the car. If the helmet came off, I wasn't allowed on the track for legal and insurance reasons. Helmet on: "Big Jew, no fit." That's Cherokee for "What the fuck was I thinking?"

❖   ❖   ❖

I'm trying to save you time, money, humiliation, and perma-nent damage to your body and ego. Like you, I wish I could hang on to my youth, adopt every non-shit-eating puppy I see, and own every hot rod known to man. But sometimes we have to know when enough is enough. Or when *none* is enough. And even if you don't listen to me, at least you can't say I didn't warn you.

21

Your Arms Are Too Short to Tickle Jesus

I don't necessarily believe in divine intervention. Though I am a firm believer in drug and alcohol intervention. Most comics have a hard time allowing themselves to get healed by the Lord because (for the most part) we're too analytical, leery, cynical, or maybe too smart to believe in something so ethereal and irrational. Or maybe we've just succumbed to the fact that we're going to hell, so why get our hopes up?

I'm a believer in evolution. And that we came from the ocean. (That's evolution, right?) My proof: sperm swims. They must know something. (That's all I got, sorry.)

The stories in the Bible certainly don't help make a case for creationism. Why they couldn't have made either Testament a tad more believable in order to get more people on the bus, I'll never know. Immaculate conception had me at the get-go. It's just another guy denying that he fucked someone. Mary was probably from the South and needed to convince Papa Drew that it was in fact a gift from the Lord or else that hussy would have seen the backside of a hand that remarkably resembled the Grand Dragon's. Joseph, poor guy, was probably black or Hispanic, and that's why there was "no room at the inn."

I believe that Jesus was nothing more than a homeless magician. That he was perhaps the first person to perfect the art of sleight of hand or close-up magic. Think about it. He had great hair and a ton of followers, turned water into wine, hosted huge suppers, traveled from town to town, walked on water, hung with a hooker, healed the sick, and always wore the same cloak. Forgive me, but this sounds a lot like David Copperfield sans the private island. His followers may have been other homeless fans or magic geeks who loved seeing the same tricks from city to city, like the first Comic Con. After all, they had no life, either.

I was raised a reformed Jew, which meant you needed to know someone to be able to score tickets for the High Holidays. According to my people, every September, God would write down everything you had done during the year and review it and get back to you. It was like an audit. Rather strange that He wouldn't wait until the end of December. Obviously, nothing ever happened to anyone, nor did we ever hear from Him. Conveniently, Jews don't believe in the devil, so why all the hype about being judged? My bubbie would say, "If God had a problem with me, I'm sure I would have heard something during Yom Kippur. After all, we had great seats. Fifth-row Torah. You could smell the blue velour."

Thank goodness Jews don't have confession. If we did, it would be called "blaming" and would be all about who *else* was at fault. It would be a three-day event just like our holidays. I was always embarrassed that my people charged their congregation members to join the temple. (I told you stereotypes have some truth.) The temple charged extra for tickets to the more popular holidays; I believe that's why they made them several days long, in order to compensate for the steep prices. Rosh Hashanah: three days. Yom Kippur: three days. Hanukkah: eight days. Passover: a week. It's like Kosher Coachella. And why? Because Jews never shut up, and we like hearing ourselves talk. Plus, the services are in Hebrew, so we never have any idea what anyone is saying, and therefore we can never challenge or deny the message, only form our own opinions.

Want to know why I toyed with Christianity and Catholicism for a while? The brevity. Christmas: one day. Easter:

one day. Ash Wednesday: one Wednesday. Midnight Mass: takes care of back-to-back trips to the church on Christmas Eve and Christmas Day. And it's all free. You throw a couple dollars into the holy basket and nobody tries to fix you up with their three-hundred-pound daughter. My friend Pat McFadden used to say, "You guys fuckin' charge people to pray? I wish we had that. Then I'd have a real reason to blow off church."

After my dad was miraculously cured from stage-three colon cancer in 1982, *without* chemotherapy and with only two days of radiation, he became a full-blown Jesus freak. The scar left by his extremely invasive surgery resembled a cross on his abdomen, and that was the only sign he needed. He started believing he had healing powers and a divine connection like no other and that he was saved by the Man Himself. He told everyone. Constantly. Especially Jews whom he felt obligated to save. That's never pretty, especially at a deli.

These behaviors unfortunately are also the hallmark of someone suffering from bipolar disorder. His religious fanaticism took a huge toll on our relationship, but we remained very close nonetheless. His myopic view of the world was predicated on religion; the Bible tainted his keen instinct and the streetwise philosophy that I always regarded as genuine and insightful. Unfortunately, our love for humor took a hit as well. The Bible just isn't funny. Making fun of the Bible is. Or was to me. When was the last time you howled at a Christian comedian? Jewish comics, on the other hand, just about invented the art.

Almost all of my later conversations with my father revolved around the Second Coming and the need to get baptized. I told him I had a huge fear of people watching me bathe and I had no idea how I'd ever allow myself to be held underwater, the by-product of watching too many Scorsese movies. My dad pressed on, and it practically drove me nuts. We were Jews. We weren't particularly good ones, but we weren't qualified to become Christians, either.

When he started to live in a trailer and eat at Wendy's, I knew it was the official end of our Judaism, though he never relinquished his sharp negotiating skills. He got thirty-three hundred dollars off on the purchase of his double-wide Teton, and the salesman showed up to his trailer park begging for four hundred back. Apparently, the guy had made a terrible mistake and sold it for just under what the dealership had paid, and his boss was going to kill him. My dad had a good heart and agreed. But only after he made the salesman listen to a thirty-minute sermon on Moses.

My father was baptized in Watts, California, in the back of some guy's office to whom he had sold hearing aids. The guy was a black preacher with a slight stutter who was between churches, and this was the only space he could get to spread his gospel. The minister used an old lobster tank he purchased from a defunct local restaurant to administer the religious dunkings. I used to tease my dad that they should have given him drawn butter instead of wine following the ceremony.

My father's dysfunctional upbringing, along with his bipolar condition and lack of judgment, was a perfect storm to become a fanatical Christian. That's why many folks find Jesus after doing prison time or waking up naked in a foreign country without knowing how they got there. It's like the classic go-to when everything else has turned to shit. I do know some truly wonderful Christians, but I notice they stop talking when I walk into the room.

I find that most people who have "turned their life over to God" are very difficult to be around. They're often controlling and judgmental, giving off the feeling that they're frozen in the 1950s with painted-on smiles and a hand in your pocket.

Growing up, I had to pray to someone. I needed help in so many areas and was so fearful of something happening to my family that I needed to cover all my bases. In temple, you're never taught how to pray. As in church, there's more cardio than connection. "Open to page fifteen, stand, sit, stand again," and repeat.

When I hit fifty, I had pretty much given up on God. I realize this looks pretty bad in print, and I'm sorry, but shit, just turn on CNN and tell me His presence isn't long overdue. Nobody has ever gotten better press than He has, but after spending half a century on Planet Blah, I have my doubts. Despite my generally skewed outlook on life, if you take into consideration all the unthinkable atrocities worldwide, it just doesn't add up. Where is He? Or She? If He can have some influence over who wins the Latin Grammys, shouldn't He be able to do something about that tornado that wiped out half a state? You can't have your Jesus-cake and eat it, too. So God, come out, come out, wherever you are! Or are we not allowed to say "come out" if we profess to be good Christians?

My father's biggest fear was having to leave me. When he was moments away from passing and his breathing was extremely labored and the pain from the cancer had created the need for huge amounts of morphine, I held his hand and said what I thought he'd want me to say: "It's okay, Dad. Don't fight. You can go to Jesus now."

His last words to me were, "Do you want me to die?"

It caught me so off guard, I was practically speechless. "Of course not, Dad. You're everything to me. I just don't want you to be in pain anymore." He never responded. How could those be his last words to me? I figured after twenty-five years of preaching the Gospel, he was ready. Then I panicked. What if he never heard my response? How could he ask that question when I idolized the man? Hopefully, he was asking my permission instead of questioning my love for him.

I'd never know. He passed away shortly after that at seventy-seven, twenty-five years after his first cancer diagnosis, when his doctors originally gave him eighteen months to three years to live. I was the only one at his bedside. I guess it was me and Dad against the world after all.

I have way too much experience with fucking cancer. I lost my amazing oldest brother, Jeff; my father; and my best friend, Ed, all within a three-and-a-half-year period, all to different types of cancer—not to mention several other loved ones and friends. My father was a huge fighter and strong as an ox mentally and physically. My brother smoked for forty years, up until the day he passed, nine months after being diagnosed, using his acerbic and brilliant humor to lead the way. My dear friend Ed had a heart of gold and lived an incredibly healthy life and fathered seven beautiful children, my godchildren; he passed way too soon. In a frightening turn of events, Ed's beautiful wife, Lorri, the sister I never had, succumbed to cancer three years after Ed. Ed and Lorri had started their own church years before and, without a doubt, were the most spiritual, kindhearted, and godly people I'd ever met.

They all took different routes of treatment, trying various combinations of chemo and radiation combined with holistic ingredients and God. These four beautiful souls had the best doctors available, and all had different opinions, philosophies, and remedies. In the end the cancer won, as it usually does.

You can "live right," "pray right," and "do right," but there are no guarantees. Ultimately, you have to live right *for you*. As in get your eyes off the clock, get off your ass, and do something good for yourself and the people around you who have your back. And keep swingin', baby.

Notice how the Jewish kids weren't allowed inside the workshop.
He insisted on meeting us on the porch.
Santa's Village, Lake Arrowhead, California, 1965.
Left to right: cousin Darren, brother Paul, me, cousin Kevin

22

Dreck the Halls

In fifty-five years on earth, I've never heard anyone say, "Boy, I sure can't wait for Hanukkah!" And that's because Hanukkah blows. Hard. Like Neil Patrick Harris after winning the Tony.

It's known as the Festival of Lights. Which are technically candles. I'm sure that would be a thrill if we hadn't had candles for the past several thousand years. Yet as Jews, we're not allowed to have pretty lights, like our gentile brethren. Unless they're blue and white, the color theme in most hospitals. And they definitely cannot be displayed on the house, because apparently, that means you believe in Jesus. Or Thomas Edison, I can't remember. But we can put a candle in the window and wait for the troops to return from the Civil War. Or light the menorah for eight nights. Wow, squeeze my nipples and call me Phyllis, is that fun. So I guess it's technically the Festival of Candles. Again, boring as shit.

Every December when I was a kid, my mom would drive me down a particular street close to our house called Candy Cane Lane just so I could eat my heart out. It consisted of about two square miles of homes that would compete every year to pull off the best damn Christmas display. And it was mind-blowing. Especially to a kid whose biggest holiday spectacle was a yarmulke that glowed in the dark. One house I'll never forget had twelve giant gingerbread men, all lit up, waving to Santa and his reindeer as they landed on the roof; all the figures moved independently. They also installed a snowmaking machine in the five days leading up to Christmas. When you see shit like that in Southern Cali, you never forget it.

I remember asking my mom once how Hanukkah began. Mom looked at me like she had just downed a bad oyster and told me "not to worry about the beginning of things but to enjoy the now." To this day I'm not sure if she was unfamiliar with the story or if she knew how lame it actually was. Excuse me while I paraphrase the parable that is Hanukkah, but I believe it has something to do with the following:

The Jewish people were once again running from some bad soldiers, known as the Maccabees, as they were migrating south to get away from the brutal winters of Mount Sinai (not the hospital). The Macs were pissed off about something and chased the Yids into a temple, ironically, where they were able to hide. The soldiers, unable to find the fleeing settlers, decided to call it a night. I don't understand how hard it is to capture people hiding in a temple, but whatever. Chances are they were huddled in the gift shop.

As folklore has it, Jews love to read before bed, but alas, they noticed there were no candles in the temple. As the more courageous Jews searched the temple for candles, they happened upon an oil lamp. One of the less intelligent Semitics rubbed the lamp, asking for better accommodations, a boat, and a referral for a good dentist.

Apparently, the oil lamp had only enough oil to keep the temple aglow for one night. Grateful that they were able to have any light at all (Festival of Lights), Mickey, the only Jew with matches, ignited the flame. And it burned for eight nights instead of one. And that's how Hanukkah was born. No manger, no Wise Men, no North Star, no Son of God, zilch livestock, not even a midget posing as an angel or elf. Just a few Jews and a lit lamp. Great story, right? Wrong. It makes zero sense and you know it.

First of all, if you're hiding from soldiers, why the fuck are you lighting the place up? You think Anne Frank thought, *I need to brighten up this attic. Someone's gonna break their neck*? Doubtful. And big deal—so the lamp burned for seven days longer than expected. A miracle? Or more like a guy who had no fuckin' idea what he was talking about and miscalculated the amount of oil. What good Jew does that? We invented calculating. Sorry, but it's no different than guessing how many jellybeans are in a milk bottle. So what makes you think you can guesstimate how long two inches of oil will last? Plus, my people seem to lean a little toward the negative side of things; expecting the oil to last only a few hours is textbook Judaism. And what rhymes with Judaism? Pessimism. I'm damn proud to be both, my friends of the goyim persuasion.

Anybody ever slip you a piece of chocolate Hanukkah gelt (money)? For those unfamiliar with the frighteningly stereotypical tradition of Jews handing out holiday chocolates *shaped like money* (HELLO?!), it must be noted that this is without a doubt the worst chocolate you've ever tasted. It typically comes from Israel, and as fabulous as they are, they're not known for their tasty confections. I keep tasting gunpowder. The crappy candy comes wrapped in a tiny pouch, like a hairnet, tied at the top. Inside are various chocolate coins wrapped in gold foil that seemed to be welded onto the stale candy discs. I remember having to sometimes bite the tinfoil off to get to the chocolate. Ever do that on a tooth filling? Put that in your dreidel and spin it.

I remember my gentile friends saying, "You're so lucky! During Hanukkah, you get gifts for eight nights!" Really? How about crap for seven nights and one cool gift on the eighth? I don't mean to sound like an ungrateful fuck, but come on! Where's all the shit under the tree, Moeshe? I mean the Hanukkah bush.

Pencils on night one. Erasers and a ruler on night two. A flashlight that would illuminate the Jewish star onto any wall on night three (more Festival of Lights; item not recommended for use while trick-or-treating). Night four, a giant chocolate coin. Slippers on night five. Night six, a year subscription to *The Shofar,* a magazine for Jewish teens with a monthly article on how to avoid bullying. Night seven, a magnifying glass and a huge pen, almost impossible to hold, that wrote in five different colors. Then there was night eight. That's when my big brother Paul would save the day. Paul always got me the best gifts, the big shit. The electric football game on the huge vibrating metal field; mini-bowling, Skittle Pool (Don Adams did the commercials); Feeley-Meeleys (pre–ShrinkyDinks); CrossFire (a game played on a slick board where you would aim a puck into the opponent's goal using steel marbles shot from a gun); Operation, Mouse Trap, and the most popular board game for Jews everywhere: Sorry!

It was nice. But it wasn't festive or celebratory or even seasonal. I wanted the gingerbread men on the lawn and those colored lights around the windows and the plastic icicles on the rain gutters. I wanted to bake butterscotch kisses for Sue and Timmy and play hide the peppermint sleigh with slow Bobby. I wanted the relatives to come by all day long and continue to drink into the night so everyone could start arguing, which would lead into racial rants about imaginary boyfriends. I yearned for the red and green neckties, the snowmen sweaters, and a kitten in a box. I dreamed of receiving a scarf made by a Southern grandma, put together from the pelts of roadkill she hit on her way to church. I wanted to know what it was like to have an Advent calendar on which, every day in December, I could open up a tiny door that hid yet another item I had no fucking need for. I wanted Uncle Ned to bring over those homemade Christmas cookies depicting the Nativity so I could bite the head off of one of the Wisemen. But most of all I wanted one sit-down with Santa. Just me and him at the mall or the tree lot. He could sit on my lap, I didn't give a shit; I wasn't in denial about my girth. I just wanted to look straight into those bourbon-ravished peepers and ask, "Why, fat man? Why did you screw the Jewish kids? Year after fuckin' year. You went to each house on either side of me, but you refused to enter the chimney from where the smell of latkes was emanating. You telling me you weren't hungry? I watched your trajectory on the eleven o'clock news, so I could see where you were on the map and at what time. I knew you blew off New Jersey, but I kept my mouth shut. And you never once showed up at Brad Gerstenfeld's. We were kids, you bloated fuck! Broken; disappointed; holding erasers and stupid flashlights toward the night sky in hopes of getting just one glimpse of ole Saint Dick." But every year he flew right by my dark, orange house with the fake candle in the window.

Guess what? It only made me stronger. And angrier. And that could be the reason I drank heavily for so many years. But age has taught me to forgive you, Jolly Jew-Hater. Just like I forgave the Maccabees for the worst holiday ever.

23

Frequent-Flyer Fuckers

With age *must* come the ability to say, "It's *my* time now," simply because your time is limited and there are no guarantees. I find this rationale to be more about becoming a survivalist than a selfish fuck, though I'm sure it's up for debate. Because I'm a big believer in fate, another cliché to consider is "If it's my time, it's my time." Obviously, this results in a drastically different outcome than "It's my time *now*," but both are beneficial to get the most from the rest of your "second half."

Here's the thing: if you find yourself on an airplane, the theory of "If it's my time, it's my time" really doesn't apply. Let's say I'm flying somewhere and it's *not* my time yet. But what about the guy sitting next to me, what if it's *his* time? Then it becomes every passenger's time, right? Ironically, this validates my philosophy as well. Do you think clean living becomes a factor when you and three hundred people are diving toward earth at warp speed? Hardly. So roll the dice with the understanding that there are many variables out there, and most work in tandem to harm you.

The only real positive of getting old is that you can board a plane early. Put on a limp and drool a little, and you'll get a row all to yourself. I don't think being obese gives you the right to board early, though. For that privilege, you should have to be handicapped, injured, or somehow incapacitated. I don't feel that "constantly hungry" quite cuts it. Please understand I have wrangled with my own weight, but there has to be a reason other than wanting first dibs on the honey-roasted snacks.

If the overweight passengers are given the right to board before everyone else, how about the grotesquely vertically challenged? Like me, for example. I didn't even make myself this way, like my fellow fatties. Do I not have the right to board early along with my competing freaks of nature? Do I not fall into the preboard, blue-card-bearing, physical-oddity section? Don't I deserve the seat with the extra legroom?

I have issues with the emergency aisles that I need to air. They are designed to give a tad more legroom when needed. And I need it. If someone is larger than I am, then they should have first dibs. It's only fair. But when I see a dwarf or a little person, gnome, jockey, Asian college student, whatever, in a seat where, if the plane stopped short, he or she would free-fall for seventy feet, it makes me think I should be sitting there. For a hundred reasons. Yes, we're both somehow physically challenged, I suppose, but I'm the one who needs the room. Hell, he could fit under the seat in front of him if he wanted, or climb into the overhead bin, the options are endless! Let the giant stretch out a touch, and maybe I'll go easy on you when I have to shoot you out of a cannon during circus week.

Also, do you realize that I am unable to sit on the toilet in an airline bathroom because my knees make it impossible to fully close the door? Neither do these grossly inadequate johns allow me to angle correctly to stand and piss. The ceiling is sloped to about six-four at its highest, which makes me have to curl my head toward my back as if trying to limbo while peeing. *Now* don't you think I should be allowed to board early?

To my girlfriend's disdain, I have zero desire to see the world. My apathy toward travel only increases with age. I just hate to fly. Or pack. Or unpack. Or wait until Sven decides whether I'm good enough to enter his stupid country. I realize it could be the twenty years I spent traveling around the country begging for yuks, that created this "bah-humfuck" attitude, but whatever. Most folks I know think I'm insane and tell me "the world has so much to offer," but in my not so humble opinion, there are no places that I feel are worth more than a five-hour flight and all the inconveniences and dread that accompany travel.

It doesn't help that I'm not very patient, and I'm spoiled. I don't like people looking through my shit, taking my cologne, asking me to take off my belt, or questioning my license photo. I'm a true believer in the comforts of home, and if "their" bed isn't as comfy as mine or the food isn't as good as the food at the places in my neighborhood, why go anywhere? If it were up to me, Columbus never would have discovered America, and look how much happier the Indians would have been, not to mention the French.

I do love architecture and museums, but I'm mainly a foodie. That's why I love New York. Five hours from L.A. Yes, there are much older buildings and better museums across the globe with astounding history, but those are often accompanied by shitty plumbing, unwashed vegetables, tiny accommodations, smelly cabbies, and languages I don't understand or want to learn. Again, smelly cabbie, only five hours away in New York.

I realize this sounds ignorant and boring to many, and that's okay. But if life is about the journey and not the destination, then travel is even more of a pant-load. If you're inclined to see the Alps, good luck to you, just please don't be the asshole who orders sushi at the airport. I see this way too often. If the friggin' hot dogs are questionable, what makes you think the ahi is the better move? Remember, food at an airport could never make it on its own on the outside. In other words, when was the last time you saw a Board of Health rating at an airport foodery? Probably never.

In my opinion, the fucked-up airlines have ruined travel. Period. The airlines are nothing more than the airborne division of the Department of Motor Vehicles. Most of the employees don't want to be there, and we're stuck with them for hours at a time while we're forced to abide by their asinine rules. And what the hell happened to the lovely stewardesses? You know, the eye candy to take your mind off the dim reality that you're floating thirty-five thousand feet above the ground in a very heavy steel tube that could be taken out at any time by a flock of fucking birds. To this day, I refuse to believe that no one has come up with a . . . I don't know, "bird guard" to keep those bastards from flying into the engines of a jet. You can hit twelve geese in a Prius and keep on going, why can't the Airbus make it through some gulls?

Stewardesses have been corporately extinct and replaced by a lower, inexpensive, unattractive species known as the "flight attendant" or "Sky Hag." In this new world of aeronautic service, the guys are prettier than the gals, and the gals are barely, well, gals. They're usually postmenopausal

heifers battling dementia who seem to juggle anger management and control issues brilliantly.

I'm writing this very chapter onboard a dumbo-jumbo
jet bound for the East Coast. (I won't say which airline, but
their initials stand for: Don't Even Leave The Airport.) A
one-way first-class seat costs twenty-two hundred dollars,
there's no Internet, the electrical outlets are nonfunction-
ing in all the seats, and the movie won't start. In 2014. And
just a few minutes earlier, the following actually happened.

The flight attendant is about seventy if she's a day, and
she's giving that tired announcement right before takeoff
that no one listens to. She seems kind of hammered, as if
she's hit a couple of those minis from the rickety beverage
cart. She slurs here and there, then repeats one part of
the announcement. The folks start looking at each other,
and I decide I'm going to open my giant piehole and ask
the other flight attendant, the buff and tanned Philippe, if
perchance his husky counterpart is hitting the sauce. After
all, we may need her assistance in an emergency, right? So
I ask Phillip with an E if Delores is drunk. And he throws
me a look that only a gay man can and replies, "She's had
a stroke."

All of a sudden "drunk" is sounding much better. I'm
sorry she had a stroke, truly. And I wish her a speedy recov-
ery. But maybe she shouldn't be on the fuckin' plane giving
directions and showing us how the oxygen masks work when
she should be the one hitting off the tank. I guess we can

thank the airline union for that one. Don't get me wrong, I'm a staunch American and I support our unions, but occasionally, they lose their sense of propriety and common sense. Sometimes you just have to thin out the herd, people. Some jobs don't mesh well with age, like anything involving moving machinery or unfurling evacuation slides. Or counting. Or hand-eye coordination, including fencing, origami, or bullfighting.

The same goes for cocktail waitresses. One of the oldest casinos in Vegas, I won't say which (rhymes with "beavers"), refuses to cut loose their elderly servers. Again, I'm all for old folks working, but if I want to see Grandma with her tits hanging out of a mini-toga, I'll go to Boca Raton.

I think flight attendants have this odd need to feel important (like DMV employees), when in reality, they know they're merely servers in the sky. Why are they so worried about my cell phone? This piece of crap can barely make a call when I'm on earth, how the hell is it going to interfere with their high-tech communication equipment in the cockpit? And don't get me started with the chair having to be "in the full upright position." What's that rationale? The wildebeest usually wakes you an hour before you have to land in order to "put your chair up."

"Why?" I once questioned when I was awakened for no reason.

"It's for your safety." She smiled.

"Explain to me the thinking behind that theory," I said.

"It's a regulation. For your safety."

"But how? How am I safer in my chair if it's barely tilted the other direction?"

"Shall I get the sky marshal to explain it?" she countered.

"You still have those? If you really want to be a crime fighter, why don't you play fifty questions with the guy in the turban and leave my friggin' chair alone?"

My point is, I'm a dick. My second point is: I guess if you're about to crash, you want to have your seat straight up instead of slightly angled by two inches. Am I the only one worried about the domino theory? It's for our safety, and some putz with an aeronautics PhD from MIT says so. I can only assume that after a plane crashes, all the different government agencies investigating gather around and try to figure out: "Who had their chair in the upright position? The black box can wait."

As you know, I only have a high school education, but if I had to pick one chair position over the other, I would definitely go with "reclined." Those passengers who *do* adjust to an upright position are obviously taller in their seats, thereby becoming more vulnerable to decapitation should the nose of the plane peel back upon impact, sending shards of debris through the fuselage. If I were reclined, all of that shit would miss me, including the unexpected fireball finale as it flies down the aisle. Who's the survivor now, bitches?

And if I have to listen to one more flight attendant bullshitting me about using my seat cushion as a flotation device, I might tape down my Sky Hag call button for the remainder of the voyage. I believe, in our lifetime, we have seen enough stories on the news about water landings. Have you ever, once, seen a passenger floating on his seat? Ever? Of course not. You know why? Because it doesn't fucking work.

The airlines are such rip-offs that even after you've paid their exorbitant ticket prices, they still find ways to nickel-and-dime you to death. Extra luggage fees? What the hell is that about? The planes are getting larger and better equipped, so why the up-your-ass charge for over-weight bags? Or extra bags? Are a dozen extra bags per flight really going to send the plane into a nosedive? If you pay for one of those ridiculously overinflated first-class tickets, shouldn't an extra bag or two be no problem? If they're worried about the actual cargo weight of the air-craft, ax three of the Sky Hags, and there's your twelve hundred pounds of free luggage. Or maybe two of those pre-boarders.

What about that insane game the luggage handlers make you play at curbside? "Oh, Mr. Garrett, one bag is fourteen pounds overweight. It'll save you fifty dollars if you can move some of the articles from this bag into that lighter bag." Huh? Sure, there's nothing I like better than opening my luggage on a filthy sidewalk so I can move my personal articles from one suitcase to another. And who cares if everyone in line gets a look at my ball-huggers with the little windmills on them, right? See, these airlines know exactly what they're doing. You pay the extra fifty bucks to spare yourself or your traveling partner that very humiliation.

My girlfriend came up with a dandy idea to keep the baggage handlers from ever stealing her high-end red-bottomed stripper heels. I never thought this was a frequently stolen item, but with what they cost, I figured maybe she was onto something. She put the left shoes in one piece of checked baggage and the right shoes in the other. This would supposedly keep them from being stolen. I promise you, she's smarter than I am and graduated with honors from McGill University, but this logic baffled the shit out of me. I have a feeling you're way ahead of me already, so I won't belabor the "strategy."

Unfortunately, one bag didn't make the connection and somehow ended up in Cincinnati as we arrived in Miami. Now my lovely lady-caller was stuck with five left shoes. Not a huge problem if you're Paul McCartney's ex-wife; I won't lie, I do find a subtle limp a bit sexy, but only if she wears an outfit that can pull it off. Unfortunately, Izzy's Jack Sparrow getup was at the cleaner's, so we were fucked.

Nowadays, even with all of our technology, there are times when they can't find the damn plane after a crash. That's because our globe is 70 percent water. And planes don't float, they fly. Usually. So if I know we're diving nose-first at 300 mph into the drink, I'm grabbing hold of the fat-ass stewardess, because she has a better chance of floating than that piece-of-crap foam cushion with the fake Navajo print. You can follow my big Jew ass off the plane, because the meek don't have a chance once those Costco oxygen masks pop from the overhead. Never seen one of those up close, but they better come with diapers tied to them.

As a side note, did you ever notice how the seat belts range in length according to what part of the country the plane is originating from? I've noticed this because I happen to have birthing hips, and on some flights I'm literally at the end of the belt. But on the flights to the South, I could tie that fucker into a bow owing to the fact that (here come the angry letters) the fatter folks originate from that part of the country. I don't mean to be offensive; again, we've established that's not my thing. It's just true. Plus, Mrs. Obama told me, and she's up on that shit. Seat belts from L.A. don't have much love for my forty-two-inch waist. New York is difficult as well. Both cities are more fashion- and health-conscious. But the belts on a flight to Louisiana? I feel petite.

Look, I don't want to discourage you from seeing the world, if that's what turns you on. But if you're like me and the best vacation you can imagine is one where you don't have to be over a mile from your own toilet, don't feel like a weirdo. You're a weirdo for plenty of other reasons, but not that one. Remember, this is your era to do what you want, when and *where* you want. You've earned the right to choose how to spend your hard-earned time and money, and if that includes telling your significant other to go to Fiji with her BFF so you can stay home with the cat, your stash of porn, and that massive log of cookie dough you got at Sam's Club, so be it. It's your time. Relish it, baby boomer.

24

Politics: Why Try?

I know this may come as a surprise after what you've just read, but with middle age, I have become increasingly fascinated by things outside of my own tiny world. Obviously, I don't feel the need to see them in person, but I am becoming increasingly nationally and globally aware. And guess what? The view sucks. Most old folks are bitter and cranky simply because all the shit that they labored over, strived for, and dreamed of never panned out. The American dream has become an oxymoron. I love my country, but it seems these days we're drowning in our own mediocrity and bullshit.

I should also mention right off the bat that I'm not politically savvy. I confuse the congress with the senate, all the old white guys in red and blue ties look the same to me, and I can't explain a caucus, though I do love saying the word. One thing I can do is watch a guy talk for ten minutes and tell you if he's full of shit or not. My batting average is most impressive. Because they are *all* full of it. They have to be to get there.

No matter how you feel about our current political situation, allow me to say a few words about the democratic system. You think your vote counts? Guess what? You're an imbecile. It doesn't. If it counted, your candidate would have won. If he or she did win, how's that going? Voting is for idiots who believe they have a voice. You know which presidents change things? The ones on the green paper. And when's the last time the Mint printed a new cash denomination to give a president props on a job well done?

We all know that the people who are powerful and smart enough to change the country don't want the gig. When is the last time you remember a president actually fixing anything? Education and illiteracy among our youth? Roads and highways? Our nation's growing poverty? Our national debt—can anyone shave a zero off that puppy? The war on terrorism? Which is as impossible to win as the war on drugs. Healthcare has finally been addressed, but I'm not sure how that will play out. Every Canadian buddy I have with a serious illness always runs over to the States, so that should tell us something about socialized medicine. How about children's rights and the astonishing number who are abused? I say life in prison, what about you? We're a nation notorious for not taking care of our own, and that's because big business runs the country, boys and girls. They've got us by the jimmies. Unfortunately, that's become the American way. Can I get a hallelujah?

Even our voting process is often a mess. The last time I voted, they told me I wasn't registered. I had proof that I *was* registered. Turned out they had my name at a different address than where I lived. In a city I'd never heard of. The volunteers at your typical polling place are around eighty-five years of age. Remember, many volunteers are people who are unable to get hired. Like at the registration desk in a hospital. They figure, "I'm so friggin' old, I might as well work at a place that has a defibrillator next to every elevator."

These polling places are more like God's waiting room. It's like old people and their parents in there, wearing their little "vote" buttons. Most have no idea how they even got to the polling place, yet they are responsible for one of the most important democratic processes we possess as Americans. Here's a good rule of thumb: if you voted for Taft, you can't volunteer on Election Day. Personally, I've voted four times in half a century. When I have, my head has protruded two feet above the booth's privacy cloth. I look like I'm in a stable.

The only candidate I ever looked in the peepers and believed was Obama. Now, not so much. I think Brother

Barack is a better human than he is a president. He seems to be lacking in the balls area. I wanted to be able to tell my grandkids, "I helped put the first black man in the White House!" But I feel the house is much whiter than he is black. I was hoping for James Brown and I got Lionel Richie, post-Commodores. This country really needed "Papa's Got a Brand New Bag" and we ended up with "Penny Lover." I would love to see President "O" go a little ghetto. Or maybe even a little Hawaii Five-O. The DNA is in there to do either or both; he just needs to dig deep and open a can of whoop-ass. Put some spice on your macadamias, my good brother, and go out like the true Chicago thug you really are.

In Obama's defense, I think that Hawaiian blood has hurt him in the long run. I love Hawaii and have vacationed there many times, but those familiar with the native people know one thing: they're slower than a shit after a cheese wheel. Their clocks don't have a minute hand. I thought we were the ones on vacation, not them. I once rented a car on Maui, and after I waited three hours for it, the manager said, "I guess my cousin Lava forgot to bring it back." Huh?

One of the biggest issues we face as a nation is terrorism. Fuckin' hate those guys. We all do. Unless you're a terrorist. It's difficult to combat an enemy who can't wait to die so he can get to heaven and have his way with seventy virgins, the assumed reward for killing the innocent and free thinking. Have you ever gotten a good look at the women who hang with Al-Qaeda? Not so purty. They wear veils for a reason, and it's not just to cover their sideburns. Put seventy of them all in one place—not exactly the Playboy Mansion.

Let's get bleaker, shall we? Global warming. Yes, it's happening. It's inevitable and unstoppable. Period. If you want to drive a Tesla because it makes you feel you're doing your part, good for you. But guess what? It won't change a damn thing. If 50 percent of the world bought Priuses tomorrow, they would have zero impact as far as repair to the ozone. If all the factories got together and made a plan, which is impossible, the ice caps wouldn't stop melting. We're in an endless game of catch-up. The hole in the sky is there to stay, and between the population's crazy expansion and the ineffectiveness of the EPA, nothing can stop the cycle. My uncle Benny's farting isn't helping matters, either.

Personally, I feel global warming is a part of our unfortunate man-made evolution. It's unstoppable, like the extinction of dinosaurs or *American Idol*. Some shit has to disappear. And one way or another, we may be next. Climate change and all its issues are bigger than humanity and larger than the good of the earth. I'm not saying any of it is acceptable or healthy, but it's all here to stay. It's the atmosphere's herpes, and let's be honest, this earth has done a lot of banging. I want a clean, green planet for my grandchildren's grandchildren, but do the math. It ain't gonna happen.

What we can do is something humans aren't very good at: prepare. Get those fucking levies and seawalls built, stat. Take in a polar bear. Invest in a company that sells tacky windbreakers or floaties. And for God's sake, if you don't know how to swim, show up at the YMCA tomorrow and sign up, anchor-ass. Who knows, maybe when it's all said and done, you'll get the waterfront property you've always wanted.

This all brings me to the topic of extinction, which could go hand in hand with the previous topic. I realize it is not good to lose a certain species of bug or owl. I get it, and I agree. It's never good news. But with three million kinds of bugs (and most of them really scary and not very useful), we'll manage. Spotted owl? Gorgeous, majestic, nocturnal . . . not the end of the world. There are one hundred and forty other kinds. Maybe not *as* spotted but definitely close, and what's wrong with stripes instead of spots? Stripes make you look taller (I should know), and maybe that's an advantage when hunting at night. Let's save the people first and then work our way down the food chain. I'm sure when the cavemen saw the last T. Rex hit the pavement, they probably uttered, "We're doomed. Who's gonna eat us now?"

In conclusion, I'm afraid to say that as a species, we're not as evolved as we think we are. I truly believe that as a group, we hit our prime in the late 1950s (except for the lack of the civil rights movement, LGBT equality, and HDTV). But that's when we started to buy our own hype, and we've been spiraling down ever since.

The good and bad news is: there's very little you can do to change anything. Aside from the impending-doom element, this should come as a relief, because it takes the pressure off. You don't have to show up and protest the building of that new Walmart next weekend. It's going to open whether you stand on the street all day with a sign or stay home and watch football. You can also put off getting those solar panels installed on your roof, or putting that candidate's sign in your yard. I don't mean to discourage all acts of goodness. Feel free to sit with an elderly person and feed him soup against his will. Or read to an undocumented child, or swerve in the road to avoid hitting a Smart car even though you really want to. Next to nothing, it's the least we can do.

25

I Hate Poker and Golf Regularly

Without a doubt, poker and golf are my two favorite sports, to watch or to play. I hyperventilate during both. The best news is that you can participate in these two wonderful games right up until you're dead. And there's a good chance that those who are middle-aged could be in their prime when it comes to these two pastimes. This is precisely why I would venture to say that more heart attacks happen on the golf course or poker table than in any other extracurricular activity.

The upside of these two sports is that it's possible for us middle-agers to defeat youngsters in either game. Therefore, if you're looking for a boost in the self-esteem area, look no further. Unless you're me. And that's where the tragedy lies. How can I be so fucking bad at poker and golf yet love them so much? It's hard to love something you suck at. Being naked comes to mind. Perhaps the reason I keep hanging on is that you need only one great shot or one great hand to get pulled right back into the torture.

What can I say about my golf game that hasn't already been documented at charity events or told with glee at country club barbecues? Maybe I enjoy golf because it gives me an opportunity to dress like a pimp. If I could only stop falling off the ball washer, I think my game would improve greatly. I just don't have the balance. Feel free to use that joke. My gift to you.

About thirteen years ago I joined a very nice country club in the San Fernando Valley that will remain nameless to protect the elderly. Let's just call it El Yewish, which means "the Jew" in Spanish. It's one of the most beautiful courses in Southern California, and when I joined fifteen years ago, I brought the average age of the members down to eighty-three. And the average round up to 118. I've been in the locker room twice in all these years; if you've never seen corpses naked and walking around, this is the place. It makes sense that lockers are left wide open, because people flee in terror. It's like *The Walking Dead* meets *Cocoon*. The upside is that the food is really good there, and when you play like me, it's all about the food anyway. I highly recommend the turkey salad, an iced tea, and a caddy named Rambo if he hasn't been deported.

I played one of my best practical jokes at El Yewish about four years ago. There was a rumor that one of the elderly members had a heart attack while at the buffet; when he keeled over, his head hit the sneeze guard on the salad bar, and his glass eye popped out. A buddy who's a member told me this story in front of my kids during a Sunday brunch at the club. Needless to say, the kids were totally grossed out. I'm not much of a practical joker, but when no one was looking, I grabbed a litchi fruit (which looks very much like an eyeball) and stuck a red bean in the hole in the middle. I swear this idea came to me because I was hallucinating from all the mercury in the whitefish. I then gingerly placed my creation on top of the croutons and began to scream. Anywhere else, this would cause a commotion, but since most of the diners were deaf, it didn't have much of an impact. My kids ran over, went white, and squealed for ten seconds until they realized what it was. They then proceeded to tell me to grow up. At age fifty, I discovered that as a father, I had turned the corner from hysterical to corny in the eyes of my kids. It happens to every dad at some point in the preteen years. My favorite audience was about to move on to hipper ground.

For those of you familiar with the game of golf and the pro/celebrity element that often surrounds the sport, let me cut to the chase: I'm the only person ever to be beaten by Charles Barkley on national television. That's saying a lot about how much I stink. Mr. Barkley, whom I have great respect for because I know he can cause me great harm, has a golf swing that is famous for its utter lack of grace or anything that resembles a fluid motion. It's almost as if he's getting struck by lightning in the middle of his back-swing: he freezes, then remembers where he is, blows off the smoke, and continues through as if only suffering a mild stroke. And he beat me. On NBC's well-known pro-athlete/celebrity golf tournament in Lake Tahoe, Nevada. I was the first player to fall to Mr. Barkley's wrath, at least on national television.

After day one of the tournament, I was next to last in the field, just edging out Charles. Day two, I took five sevens and two tens on various holes. You heard me. I was wearing the Ping golf hat that came in the gift bag, and after day two, a representative from Ping kindly asked me to remove it because the tournament was being televised. Then a rep from Titleist approached me and said he would send me a free set of clubs if I didn't wear their shirt. This may have been the first and only request for *lack* of celeb-rity endorsement for any product, ever. So instead I wore a baseball cap from Brent's Deli, one of my favorite eater-ies, and turned my shirt inside out. I figured my pals at the deli would appreciate the exposure. Apparently not. My favorite waitress, Shirley, avoided me like the plague after that, saying she wasn't allowed to wait on me because I five-putted wearing their hat.

By the end of day three, Charles beat me by, I believe, six strokes. I can't remember, exactly. I stopped keeping score when I was lying sixty after nine holes. Romano and I played in the same foursome that weekend, and when a reporter went up to him and asked, "How does Brad shoot a sixty after *nine holes*?," Ray quipped back, "Well, it appears he missed the putt for fifty-nine." And that's why everyone loves him.

My sweet revenge on Sir Charles came a few years later at the Ante Up for Africa charity poker event in Vegas, hosted by Don Cheadle and Matt Damon, where I took him out in a friendly game of Texas Hold 'em. It was a wonderful one-two punch. First I took him out with trips over his two pair. He immediately rebought; the very next hand he had pocket kings and went all-in, and I "rivered" him, making a gutshot straight to knock him out again. I have a great picture of it hanging in my office. Maybe one day I'll have the balls to ask him to sign it.

Gambling in general is loved by many, but it's especially appealing to the old fucks. I imagine this is because they figure, "What have I got to lose that I haven't lost already? I can't hear, can barely see, can't taste, can't remember shit, have trouble walking, am wearing a diaper, and nobody comes to visit unless they have a gurney." Putting eight hundred bucks on 29 black has a whole different meaning when you're waiting for a liver transplant. Which reminds me of one of my favorite gambling stories of all time. This one didn't even involve me directly.

It was a good twenty years ago, and I was working in Vegas. I was nursing a hangover during the day while playing a quarter video poker machine. An older couple was playing the new Megabucks slot machine a few feet away from me. Megabucks was relatively new back then, and like most people, they didn't realize that the odds were grossly stacked against them (like in most casino games). This was also a game that offered the possibility of winning millions by slipping two dollars into the ole slotsky. The Megabucks machines are tied into all the other Megabucks machines in all the casinos around the country, including Reno, Atlantic City, Tahoe, etc. Most people didn't know that, especially back then. This is how the huge payouts were possible and also why the odds of your machine hitting were even more remote.

This forever-married couple was bickering with every spin. It was annoying and lovely at the same time. She kept grinding on him for putting in two coins with every spin, as opposed to one. He tried to explain that you win the millions only if two coins are played. She proceeded to call him "dim-witted" for believing he could actually hit the mega-jackpot. Her plan was to play it safe and get more spins by playing one dollar at a time, which in all actuality could win them ten thousand dollars with the same three tiny rainbows appearing. A long shot as well, but more probable, according to the broad. And as we know, they're usually right. "Quit being a nutcracker," the husband squawked, with a Pall Mall dangling from his five teeth.

"I thought we agreed to only gamble at night," she replied.

"When did we say that? You're dragging me to Engelbert later." He then told her that he had to go "take a leak," but he was feeling lucky and wanted her to continue playing the machine. He made her promise to use two coins. She said okay. He made her *swear*. She stared at him the way only a long-suffering wife can as "I swear" dribbled from her overly glossed yapper. The old man gave her the plastic bucket of silver dollars and crossed into the john as she continued to play the machine with a look on her face like they may both end up homeless.

I was playing my quarter poker when all of a sudden I heard bells and whistles going off like I've never heard to this day. I glanced over to see the nutcracker screaming and jumping up and down. Everyone in the casino came running over. I got up and walked over to their machine as well. The chimes were deafening while the three rainbows illuminated in all their glory. She had hit it. The husband came running from the bathroom, screaming, while trying to pull up his stuck zipper. It was mayhem as the couple embraced and attempted to jump up and down as if they were young lovers again. The husband with the wet spot on his Sansabelt trousers looked up in utter joy and saw "$10,000" lit up and flashing on top of the machine. He froze. The number above the ten grand, the "$1,548,072," was not lit up. Nor flashing. The crowd took this in simultaneously as the poor son of a bitch turned to his wife. He got pale and wobbled ever so slightly. Just then a casino host whispered, "She only put in one coin?" The crowd gasped, but the wife continued to gloat.

"What? We won ten grand, Bernard!" she said. The celebrating came to an abrupt halt. The casino revelers began to disperse. The husband slowly reached out, but not with a congratulatory embrace. The defendant began to almost unconsciously strangle his wife. Not maliciously; almost as something he must do. A duty. It was pathetic from both perspectives, but it took five security guards to pull this sixty-eight-year-old man off his wife as his breakdown began. "One fucking dollar, you no-good whore! One fucking dollar and our lives would be as we had always dreamed!" resonated through the casino. It was as if Shakespeare wrote a casino tragedy for the 1980s, and I was one of the chorus taking it all in.

The husband spent the night in jail, and the wife went shopping. Most likely for a turtleneck sweater to cover her one-dollar bruise. Or perhaps she spent some money on a restraining order. One fucking dollar was the difference between ten grand and one and a half million. Or was it? Would the rainbows still have shown up if two coins were inserted? Who knows. Gambling experts say yes, while conspiracy theorists say no. But the point is much bigger than that. The wife had to do it her way. Granted, her innate frugality had probably kept them afloat for many years. But in my gut, I know they divorced after that event, because a guy can never let that go, I'm sorry to say. Then again, if he had won the $1.5 million, he could have split anyway. Or maybe she would have been the one to go. Blend together alcohol, money, lack of sleep, and a couple's dynamics, and you will see the best fights in Vegas outside of the ring.

In over thirty years of playing the casinos, I can tell you that I've lost significantly more than I've won. As in an embarrassing amount. I have the addictive behavior that feeds on games of chance. Add to that the quality that makes all artists dreamers, along with a love for life on the edge (which most comedians have), and the result is a perfect storm. Presently, I gamble about one tenth as much as I did in my crazy days, but it's not uncommon to see me at a roulette wheel or at a low-stakes no-limit Hold 'em game in Vegas.

I love poker best, and the loudmouth you've maybe seen on ESPN during the World Series of Poker Main Event is more my TV table persona while the cameras are rolling. I have a much quieter demeanor when I'm sitting in a corner at a table in Aria or the MGM Grand in Vegas (where my comedy club is located). As I like to say, "If you have no game, try putting them on tilt."

My cousin Darren, a stealth player, got me into his poker

game thirty years ago, and that morphed into two other home games with "The Poker Joes." One consists of my close friends from eons ago; the other is always with Romano and is visited frequently by Jason Alexander, Cheryl Hines, Teri Hatcher, director Rob Schiller, and various attorneys and business managers. These are all folks who take my money home pretty regularly. I also find women to be some of the best poker players out there. They have all the necessary ingredients to win: patience, the inability for us to know what the fuck they're thinking, and tits.

I use poker as a release from the grind of my business. If I use something so unstable to relax, you can only imagine my daily biorhythms, but trying to figure out the cards helps me forget the other crap rolling around in my skull. The problem is, I'm not patient in general, and that quality is crucial in order to have a strong game. And I suck at math. And get bored easily. Usually, I'm simultaneously doing emails. So why do I play? Simply to meet Asian men, I suppose. They fascinate me.

I was once taking private lessons from poker pro Annie Duke, whom I defeated, ironically, on the NBC Heads-Up Poker program a couple years prior to hiring her for coaching. This proves what I've always said: "You need the cards to win. Period." I'll take luck over skill any day. Duke can typically beat me with her eyes closed.

After my fourth lesson with Annie, I noticed that she was hitting a crucial level of mathematical reasoning I just couldn't grasp. It was taking too much effort, and that was zapping the fun out of the game. Most great poker players are mathematical geniuses on one level or another. But at the end of the day, they're no different from your average degenerate gambler trying to churn out a living. I couldn't imagine anything harder.

26

Why Fame Sucks

I don't want to come off as an ungrateful whiner, but I'm afraid that ship has already sailed. I use the word "fame" loosely here, because in all honesty, my career is at the point where about half of the people who recognize me think I'm Kramer from *Seinfeld*. Especially Mexicans. I'm not sure why that is, but I think it could be the same reason why white people mistake Morgan Freeman for Samuel L. Jackson. Or the guy on the Cream of Wheat box.

"Fame" and "celebrity" feel like dirty words these days, especially when they're attributed to people who are mostly talentless, like Paris Hilton, the Kardashians, or the Real Housewives of Wherever. Sure, people "love" them and are enamored by their lifestyle as opposed to their ability, and that's fine. I just wish they weren't clumped into the same category as theatrical or musical artists who spend their entire life working on their craft. These reality stars (who are anything but real) should be grouped in with celebrity impersonators, carnival sideshows, and wax museum figures, then sealed in a time capsule with the words *When Shit Went Wrong on Earth* written on it.

The paparazzi are among the pariahs in the entertainment industry who fuel these attention-starved individuals. The death of Princess Diana, for example, could have been avoided if someone had policed these bums like they would if a non-celebrity were being pursued or stalked. That's the part of fame that is most frustrating of all: the famous are not treated equally under the law. I know, "Boo-hoo, you fuckin' stars," right? But hear me out.

Several years ago the paparazzi routinely followed me from one location to another when I was with my children, oftentimes scaring them. These are not always polite photo-taking individuals. They are aggressive, invasive, provocative, and often work in herds. If I were a dentist or a plumber and some dumbshit was hiding in my bushes taking pictures of me and my children in the backyard, I assume there would be legal repercussions. If a total stranger is taking pictures of your kid who happens to be a minor, you'll want to shove something far into his ass, won't you? Especially in this day and age?

Unfortunately, there was an incident when I let the

papa-Nazis get the better of me. I had just started dating my girlfriend, IsaBeall, and we were leaving the popular Beverly Hills eatery Dan Tana's. I had just polished off a great chicken Parmesan and was tired and not in the mood for the paparazzi bullshit. As we stepped out the front door, about twenty people surrounded us with bulbs flashing, some yelling, "Pin them in! Don't let them out!" as we waited to get our cars. My girlfriend and I decided to go down an alley to avoid them; they followed and got between me and my car with their video lamps blaring and their asinine questions spewing. So I gingerly moved a camera out of my way. Gingerly like a bear taking a swipe at a maggot on his nutsack. That led to some strong words, and we all know if the cameras weren't gathering potential evidence, none of these punks would have the balls to approach their grandma at a picnic, let alone people in an alley. I think I bent one of the lenses or some bullshit. They tried to press charges, but the local DA was intelligent enough to view the footage and realize these guys were being annoying assholes, and the charges were dropped.

I'm not a violent guy. I've been in only two fights in my entire life, including one in fifth grade, when tiny Dicky Pargolis took me out with one shove in a David-and-Goliath moment. But I'm protective when I feel I or the people I'm with are being taken advantage of or disrespected. Interestingly enough, with my newfound middle-age maturity, I realize they don't deserve the beating I'd love to give them because that would only bring attention *to them,* plus the legal shit and possible settlement that they hope to encounter in order to pay their rent. These scumbags prey on people in their worst hours, be it rehab, a courtroom, or a place they maybe shouldn't be in a certain condition.

This is why I hate Twitter and Facebook as well. I realize that most people in showbiz use social media as a publicity tool, and that's their prerogative, but I just don't think that everyone has to hear from us all the time. No matter who we are. Mainly, I don't think I'm so important that people need or care to hear what I'm doing every waking moment. I bore the fuck out of myself; I don't think you need to hear how my colonoscopy went or which restaurant I think has the best gnocchi. My comedy club has a Facebook page for business purposes, but I don't personally have one because there's a lot of my past I want to leave there, and I feel like shit for not friending people I didn't want to be friends with anyway. I just can't afford any extra guilt. Again, for me, it's all about holding on to any kind of privacy or anonymity, which is extra difficult at six-eight.

I had a Twitter account a few years back, when a PR firm took me kicking and screaming into the fray of social media. I hated it and closed it within seventy-two hours. Here was my dilemma: first, it felt wrong having someone run it for me. When I ran it myself, I wasn't interested in responding to the majority of my 172 followers. If I *did* respond, I had engaged myself and must continue, but I was likely to end up either saying something too honest or inappropriate (like I always do), which would piss someone off, or not responding at all and then looking like a dick. So what did that leave? My telling the handful of folks that I would be performing at the Gag Silo in Muncie, Indiana, the following weekend, and who cared about that?

It seems that with celebrity, you have somehow agreed to forfeit all of the privacy that is guaranteed in the Constitution. I once had a very high-profile entertainment attorney tell me, "The public has a right to you because you are a known performer." I don't agree with that, and I'm proud that my fellow thespians with bigger names and giant clout are attempting to enforce change. I'm enough of a realist to understand that's probably unlikely, because we all know that exploitation is big business, and greed is king, and people are dumb enough to read or view the tabloid crap and think it's real. Or, even worse, relevant.

If only the public understood that these rags are mostly stories cultivated from lies and conjecture, accompanied by photos that have been changed or doctored. But people love to feel they have a connection to their celebrities and artists, and I can appreciate that. Many envy our lives without knowing anything about them, and simultaneously love watching us stumble or fail. I need to keep reminding myself that we sell escapism, and that includes giving people the ability to feel superior or akin to us.

Probably the biggest challenge for anyone who acquires

any degree of fame is doubting the sincerity and attraction from other people. Are they in it for me? Would they date me if I didn't know Tootie from *Facts of Life*? Are they being friendly only because I host Iguana Week on Animal Planet? Are they breaking up with me because they saw my scene in *Sharknado*? And so on. People are generally insecure, and adding the element of celebrity only makes one more leery and defensive, and rightfully so. Personally, I've used it to my advantage, and I'm not too proud to admit that. It has definitely gotten me laid, and it's backfired only once.

Back when I was opening for Sinatra, I brought a hot blonde to Vegas with me to watch the show. I was praying I could arrange a quick hello from the man himself to impress my date, as I had been opening for Frank for about eighteen months and he was really cool with me hanging around. After my set that night when I walked offstage, out of the blue, Frank said to me, "Come by after the show to my dressing room. We're gonna have some pizza from Patsy's."

"Sounds great, Mr. S. Thanks!" I replied. My plan was on its way to working, and all I could think about was that blonde's rack on my head.

After the show, I proudly took my gal by the arm and went to knock on the door with the gold S on it. Frank opened it up wearing his robe, looked me straight in the eyes, and said, "Whataya want?"

"Too early?" I asked.

"For what?" he replied.

"Dinner?" creaked out. Sinatra just stood there, smiled, and closed the door. He had forgotten he'd invited me just two hours earlier. Either that or he had a hot blonde in there, too. My date just glared at me. I countered with "Wanna meet Frank Jr.?"

There is something important that I think you civilians out there need to understand, and that is: stop expecting athletes, singers, actors, TV ministers, wrestlers, talking animals, or Paula Deen to be role models for you or your children. We didn't aspire to be artists in order to become role models, so get a life and be a role model *yourself* instead of expecting some talentless fuck from a boy band battling puberty to set a good example for your child. Roll up your sleeves and parent with honesty and integrity; show your kids that talent and recognition don't always go along with humility and wise choices. Granted, those of us who strive for this business are individuals who want to be noticed and hopefully looked up to, but sometimes we're less examples of how to behave in society and more reflections of that same society, bad or good.

I owe so much to my fans. All 172 of them. Any performer worth his weight in antidepressants will tell you, "We're nowhere without YOU." From the folks who used to watch me at the Ice House in the eighties and say, "I can't believe I paid a whole seven dollars for this," to the people who show up today in Vegas at my club in the basement, or in the audiences of one of my soon-to-be-canceled sitcoms: you have never gone unnoticed or unappreciated.

I always try to take a minute to chat or do a picture when asked, because I should. And usually want to. I feel it's a small price to pay for an extraordinary life. Unfortunately, sometimes I have to say no, and I'm sorry. Like when I'm at a urinal; buying porn; with someone I shouldn't be with; have the runs; about to miss a flight; wearing someone else's pants; fleeing from a large black man who was sitting in the front row of my show; or if you smell like vomit (Reno, Nevada); and so forth. But I always try. And I will never take for granted the fact that the same people who yell "Kramer" in Spanish (also pronounced "Kramer") are the ones who watched *Raymond* reruns in Argentina, Hacienda Heights, and around the world.

It is time that has made the public's recognition wane, and it's not their fault. Just like it is time that has made me forget the name of my youngest nephew. And in a few years, I may be recognizable only to the folks I owe money to. It's all good, because at one time I was known as "Raymond's brother, Robert," and that's good enough for me. It's given me a wonderful and fulfilling life.

Just the other day a guy yelled, "Hey, Robert!" from a passing car as I was walking down the street. I yelled back, "Hey, viewer!" He laughed and yelled back, "Loved you on *Friends*!" Hey, I'll take what I can get.

27

Dirt Nap for Daddy

Personally, I have zero fear of dying alone. I actually demand it, and you should, too. It's even in my Living Trust. The minute papa can't open his peepers, all must head for the lobby. I hate it if someone just watches me sleep, so you can imagine having someone watch me die would be a fate worse than death. I don't want some dame standing over me with a mirror held up to my mouth with one hand and a will in the other. We entered the world alone, and that's the way we should go out. A group holding vigil around the adjustable deathbed makes no sense and is creepy for everyone. Say goodbye before the morphine runs out, and remember me with my eyes open and mouth agape.

As you can probably tell, I try not to live in the past or the distant future. I'm a big believer in moving on, and I find reminiscing pathetic, a silly pastime reserved for the elderly as they muddle through dementia, waiting for the bimonthly visit from their ungrateful bastard of a son, stroking a stuffed cat that they think is real. The thought of waiting for a nurse to stroll by and sneak me a pudding cup is why I'm a huge supporter of euthanasia. Let me donate my organs pronto so the next poor soul can give them a whirl. I'm not trying to break any records sitting in a chair unnoticed. We're allowed to let our pets die without suffering and with dignity, but humans in this country have to die a pound and a breath at a time because the God Squad says so.

As we age, we question more. I find myself doing it constantly at fifty-five. Is there a heaven? Will there ever be world peace? Does no always mean no, or could she be playing hard to get? It's all part of our undeniable evolution toward the end. The fear of dying without learning shit. The minute we finally figure something out, we're near death or can't remember what we were trying to accomplish in the first place. We're a pinched nerve away from dwelling on the meaning of life when our brain switches right into: "Why is there a smiling clown face in my dinner plate?" It's an ugly truth. The first several decades of our life are spent in a trial-and-error configuration that generally snaps back in our face as we say, "Well, that hurt. I'll never do that again." Bullshit. You'll indeed do it again, just to a different part of your body. Or to someone else's body.

As we know, with age, the body clock takes an ugly turn.

You have dinner at four-thirty P.M. Wake up at dawn. Fall asleep with your pants unbuckled in the middle of *Wheel of Fortune*. You've adopted the schedule of a farmer. It's as if the body knows you're headed toward the end, so it gets you up earlier to experience more but gets you to bed early enough to miss the eleven o'clock news.

I had a conversation the other day with my business manager of thirty years, the debonair, unshaven Joe Sweeney, because I believed I had stumbled onto a brilliant idea that could spur my early retirement. Death insurance. He said, "You mean life insurance. They already have that, schmuck."

I said, "No, asswipe. You're not hearing me. Death insurance." This would be the kind of insurance we could take out while still in our right mind; it would guarantee if and when we get MENTAL in our later life, and we either swear we are Benjamin Franklin, or are stuck daily, sitting in the window, yelling aeronautic quadrants to the approaching mother ship, that a person will have the pre-granted right to come up behind us and take out the back of our skull with a shovel. And there would be no legal ramifications for this act. I know two people in my life who will happily sign up for this job tomorrow. For free. Look at death insurance as the precursor to pulling the plug, only a lot easier on the family, because the guy with said shovel would pretty much take the lead. He's a predesignated hired hitter.

I'll never forget when I was much younger and I visited my grandmother in a home. She was pretty much gone at that point. She had started calling me Craig, which I actually didn't mind.

Anyhoo, there was this really old gentleman who would sit in his wheelchair facing a particular corner of the cafeteria, yelling random "winning" lottery numbers. Every day. From dinnertime (three-thirty P.M.) until bedtime, one group of numbers after another. "Here we go, everyone, and good luck! Ten, fourteen, seven, twenty-two," and so on. I loved it. Even more than seeing my grandma. It fascinated me and made me bust a gut simultaneously. Most visitors found it sad, but being a sick gambler deep down, I would often jot down the numbers and play them that week in the lotto, just in case the gentleman was onto something. Ironically, the other confused patients at Northbound Horizons also thought an actual bingo game was in progress and would badger the nurses for bingo cards and markers that did not exist. This often caused a melee of walkers and scooters embarking into the lobby and demanding to be part of the game.

Ultimately, this country has zero dignity for the elderly when "the captain has left the bridge." The last thing we want to be is a burden to our children, yet we know damn well we will most likely become exactly that. Some of us feel it's only fair because of what they did to us as teenagers. But as I always say, "If I don't know where I am, I sure the fuck don't want to be there." Period. No matter how great the hot cocoa is. It's hard enough at this stage of my life to accept the fact that the glasses I'm looking for are on top of my head.

There is one point I must make for the sake of safety: you old fucks must relinquish your car keys. Sooner rather than later, please. We get it. You drove one of the first Model T's, and now you're driving a rocket-powered Chrysler 300, and it's the shit. However, I feel that people over eighty should not be allowed to drive. Ever. The car should be taken away, and they should be demoted to one of those red scooters I see darting through the casinos in Vegas with blue-haired abandon. This should be a wake-up call, people. Since they can barely drive those three-wheelers, why would we let them continue to drive a mass of steel weighing two tons? At least when they pass out on a scooter, it slows to a stop and, worst-case scenario, they bump into a buffet line or a night nurse. I don't give a crap if Grandma beats everyone at *Jeopardy!* or not. Just because she's nailing questions about Teddy Roosevelt, all cozy in her La-Z-Boy while hitting off the oxygen, doesn't make her freeway-eligible. We don't care if she double-dated with Lewis and Clark or not. Stay off the fuckin' road, Nana. If you need a magnifying glass to do the word jumble, we don't need you merging on the 405 freeway, unable to turn your head sufficiently because your carotid artery has more crud in it than a Lady Gaga pap smear and your reflexes left with the Johnson administration. And since you're old as dirt, you want to be waited on, right? Shit, you've earned it! Let Rosa drive you to the store, or call one of those white senior vans I get stuck behind every Friday at rush hour. Sit back, take your teeth out, and relax. Driving is not your last independent privilege. Opting not to kill your fellow man at a farmers' market is. In other words, P will always be Park. And D will always be Drive. But R does not stand for Race. Don't clown it, Gramps. Give us your keys.

Me as the old Jackie on the set of *Gleason*, Montreal 2000.

28

Fifty Is the Old Thirty

Well, this is it. You've made it to the end of the book, and I'd like to thank you for sticking with me. I hope that by now you feel a little freer, a little less burdened by life, and a little more able to be your *true* self, whatever that means. My goal has been to give those of you who are either facing, in the midst of, or long past middle age, the permission to do what the hell you want. You have probably realized that getting in shape, eating right, building up your spouse, achieving more success, understanding your kids, and rescuing the ozone are grossly overrated. And you usually end up unfulfilled and overstressed in the process.

However, I can't discount the one benefit of stress: it's

become my only cardio. I actually feel somewhat healthy, so my overreacting, high anxiety, and obsessing must be good for something. Or maybe I just have good genes, because as you know I don't eat right and I don't work out. Which again proves my point: what are we really in control of? Zip. Here's to embracing your anxiety just enough to bump up the endorphins so you can blow off the gym. As I always say, the difference between an anxiety attack and a heart attack is an apple fritter. Supposedly, God lives in the details, so good luck to you. Hopefully, He's home when you can't feel your left arm.

The time is *now,* my high-cholesterol friend. This is true no matter what age you are, but absorb it with more haste if you're getting up three times a night to pee. "Been there, done that" is your new mantra and is permission to follow your desires—or not. Both are fine. If you want to take that AbBuster you bought six years ago (and the Total Gym you bought two years before that, and the *Buns of Steel* tapes you got in 1991) and have a bonfire in the backyard, you go for it. You want to take up two parking spaces because your blood thinner is off-kilter and things look fuzzy? Be my guest. You want to cock-block your acid reflux and take some preemptive antacids prior to your visit to the Korean barbecue? Rock the baby backs, you pathetic and fearless old fart, because the world is your ointment.

Truth be known, there isn't any part of my life I'd want to revisit. I'm the happiest I've ever been right now. Okay, that's not true, but I've decided to believe it anyway. And that's a conscious choice we all have to make. How, you might ask? By remembering to be genuinely grateful for the life you lead. By accepting yourself and those around you and trying to approach others with compassion and respect. By trying to be transparent to yourself and your loved ones. I'm not going to say I have no regrets, because that's horse-shit, but knowing the feeling of my present contentment, I can only view my past mistakes as part of the path that got me here today. Yes, there are always going to be days that suck beyond belief, and things will happen that are beyond your control. For those occasions, you need the balls and the belief in yourself to trudge through.

In my life, I've been richer and more successful than I am right now, but some of those years were also my darkest. There are times when I long for the energy of my youth; the rush that came with every new gig; the euphoric high of falling in love; the freedom of living like an animal with my buds, while knowing I could move back in with my folks if I ran out of bread; the days when two martinis did it; that one year when I was a "normal size" and had a dozen jeans to choose from at the Denim Barn; not to mention the mind-less hard-ons that would appear out of thin air. But with all of that came an unforgiving, inexperienced ignorance, and I had to learn many life lessons along the way that I wouldn't want to go through again. I don't miss any of that at all today. Well, maybe the mindless hard-ons. And the euphoria. And the selection of jeans and living like an animal. Fuck, I'm lying again.

If I know anything, it's that we must continue to evolve, especially emotionally and in our desire to discover. Not to stay young but simply to age with some damn purpose. We can slow down, people, without slowing up. As Sinatra used to say, "I've been down but never out." And that philosophy is ageless. Because come Monday, you're just another Joe one step ahead of the guy with the shovel.

Well, I'm out of words. Writing this book, while cathartic, has been one of the most difficult things I've ever done. I feel like I'm two sentences away from pissing blood. So allow me to say in closing: may all your colonoscopies be negative and may your last marriage be with a nonspeaking pole dancer from Prague. And just promise me you won't fall victim to a phrase like "Age is wasted on the old." Because if that happens, it would not only be a shame, it would prove you haven't learned a fucking thing from my rambling tirades and bad credit. Which, with my history, could possibly throw me into a late-life crisis. And nobody wants to read about that.

Acknowledgments

There are too many to name especially since my memory is beginning to blow. I'm sorry if this looks like it's listed in order of importance. Only part of it is, so get over it. So many played a part in my crazy life. You know who you are but if I happen to forget you, forgive me.

Special thanks to my children Max and Hope, who make it clear every day why I love being here; IsaBeall Quella, my last true love; Mom and Dad for giving me the freedom and belief to try shit while learning to be fearless; brother Paul for always having my back; brother Jeff—miss you every day and thanks for teaching me the joy of sarcasm. Ina Maus, Lionel—for helping me with my first monologue; Sean and Chris, Eddie C. Sr. and his Lorri, DC and the poker Joes, The White Knight, Ruby, Eryn Brown—my dedicated manager who forced me to write this book; Eric Kranzler & Mgt 360, Scott

Schachter for giving it a go, UTA, Steve Levine, Daniel Greenberg, WJ Meade, Divorced dads who show up, Bobby Conti, Kimberley Evans, The Manfredis, Mean Chicken Lady, Pat Fraley, Carole Fisher, Sandy Bush (not the porno star but my high school Spanish teacher at El Camino Real High School in Woodland Hills), the broads at Gallery Books, Steve Altman, Jayson Cohen, Chic and Patti Perrin & The Indianapolis Comedy Connection, Bob Fisher & The Ice House, The Laff Stops, The Improv on Melrose (not the one in Houston that tried to stiff me), Howard Trustman, The Comedy & Magic Club, Adam Silver, Thom Rollerson, Lee Wilkof, Manfro, Richard Sturm, Wesley Wofford, Bob & Tom of Indy; Prof. Adam Hill, my friends at MGM Resorts, Ed Wiley, Bob Wolfson, Hubie Brooks, Rick Jackson, The Buelows, Olaf, Anthony Jackson, Cliffy-Kim, Joseph "Van Buren" Sweeney, Larry Babitz, Nathan Horwitz, Michael Gendler, my peeps at the BGCC, Kat, April Winchell, Walnut Garden, Finchetta, Will McGuire, Steve Stark, Roy Stark, Sam Katz & Winnepeg, Lynda McCarrell, Butchie, Twin Dragon, NYPD, Dr. Richard Wulfsberg, Dr. Sam Spiegelman, Nathan Lane, Mooney, Jason Alexander, Whoop, David E. Kelley, Dave Boone, Richard Lewis, Kevin Nealon, Tony Camacho, my Seven Godchildren, Donovan Cook, John Fox, Bill Kopp, John Lassiter, John "Kats", Jamie Thomason, The Laugh Factory, Tommy Koenig, R.W.—RIP, Coach Dick Bone (not a typo), Southern Cali; and to all the dives, theaters, and clubs across America and Canada that let big mouths like me open wide.